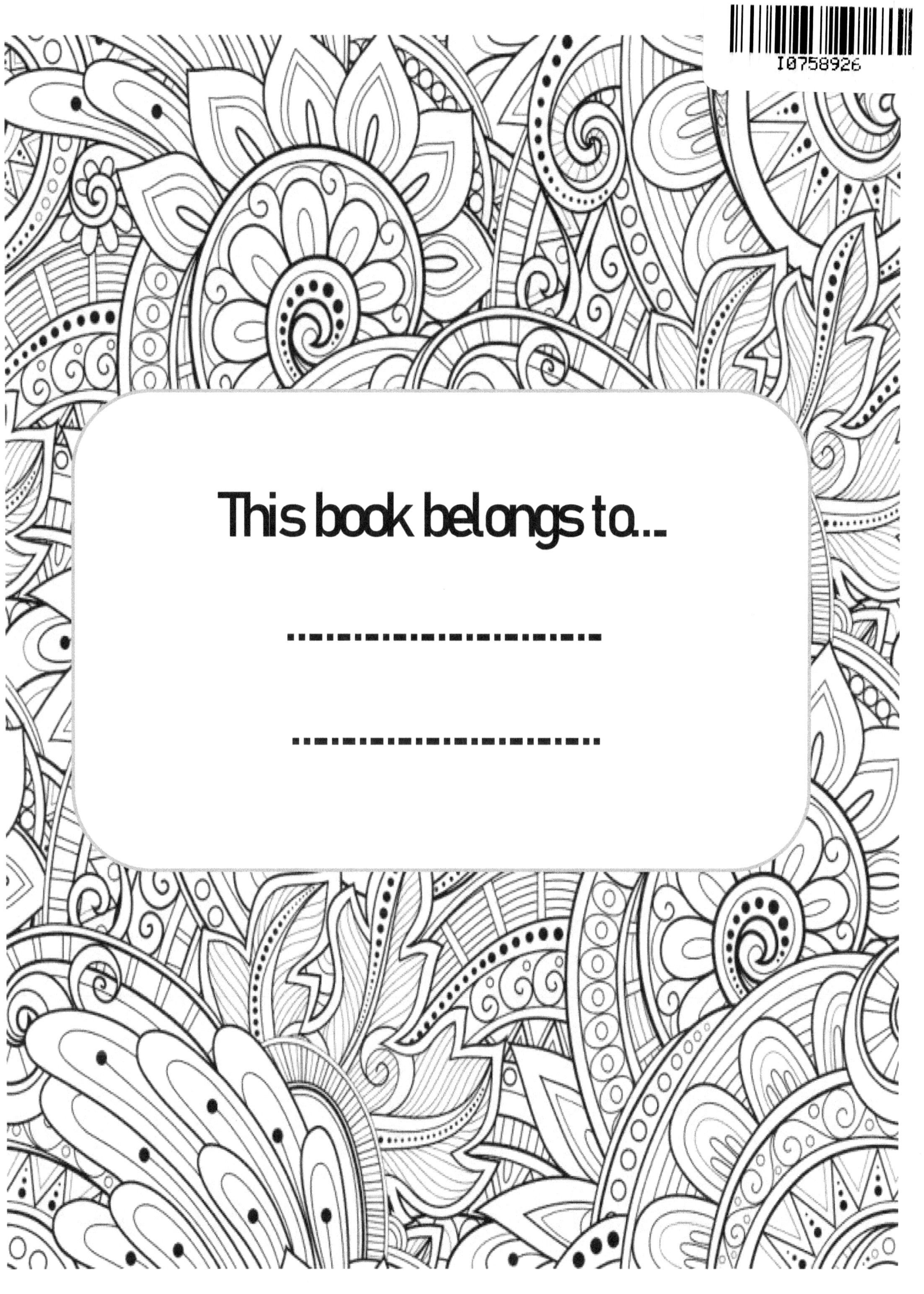

This book belongs to...

Sample of designs

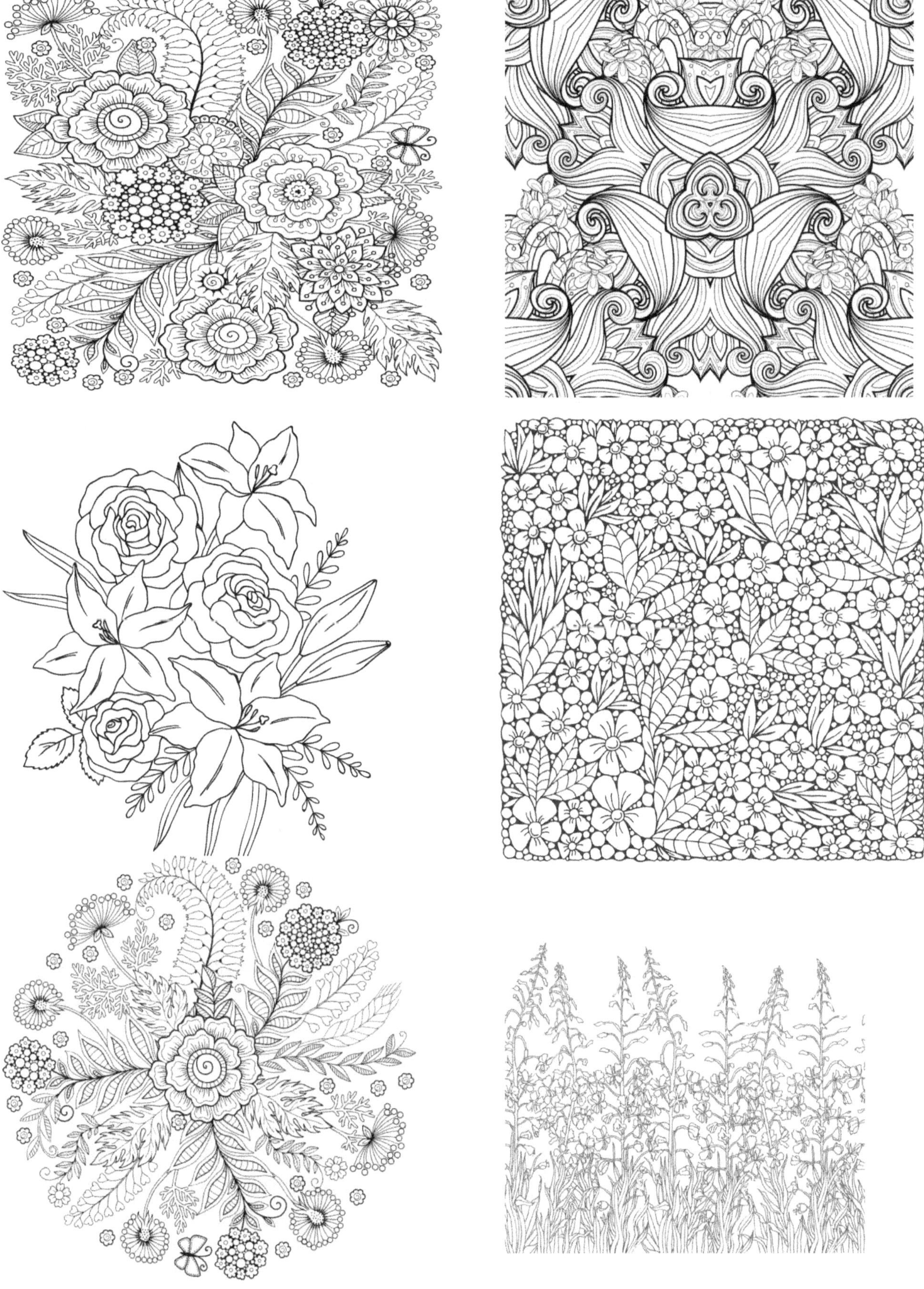

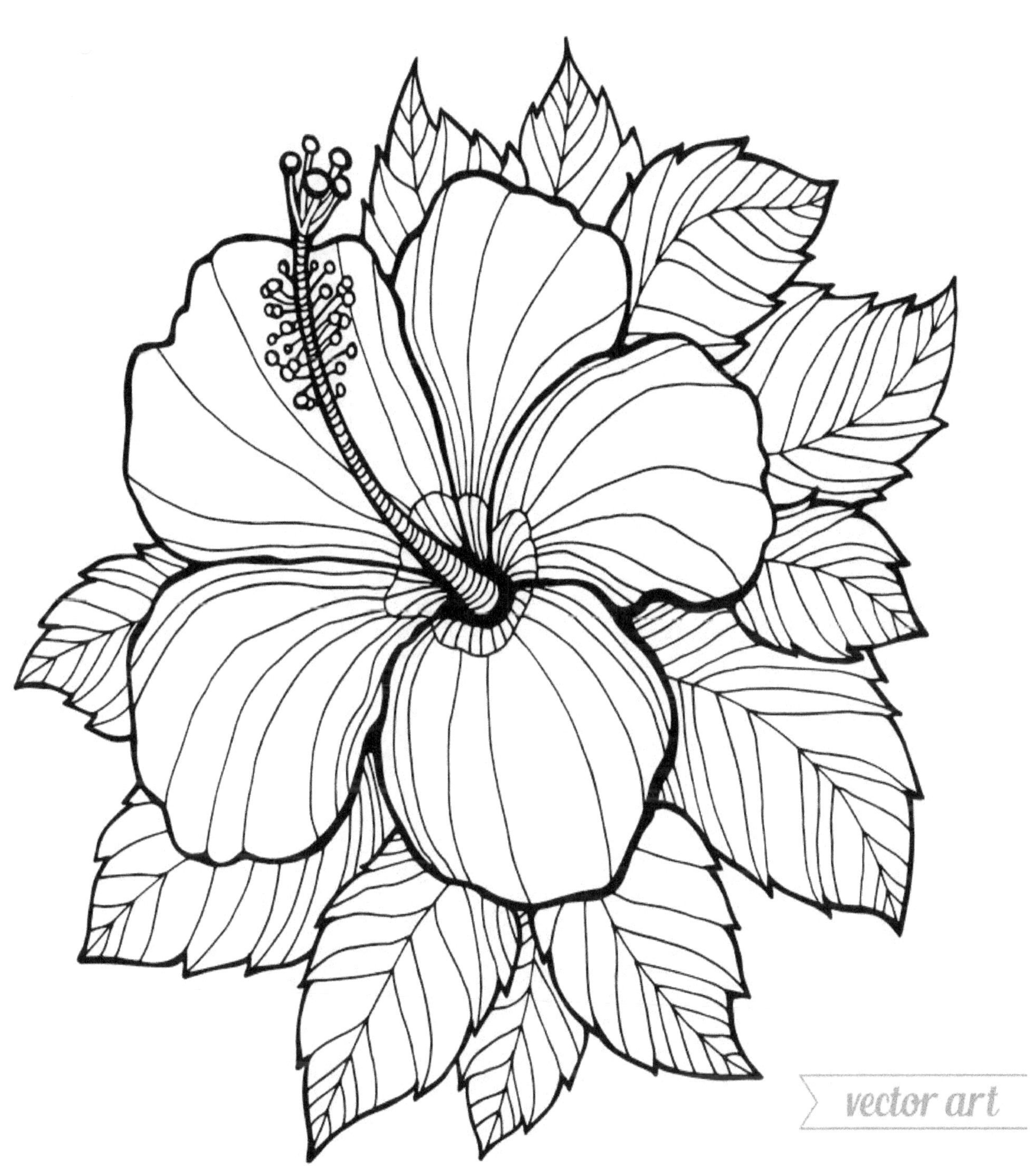
vector art

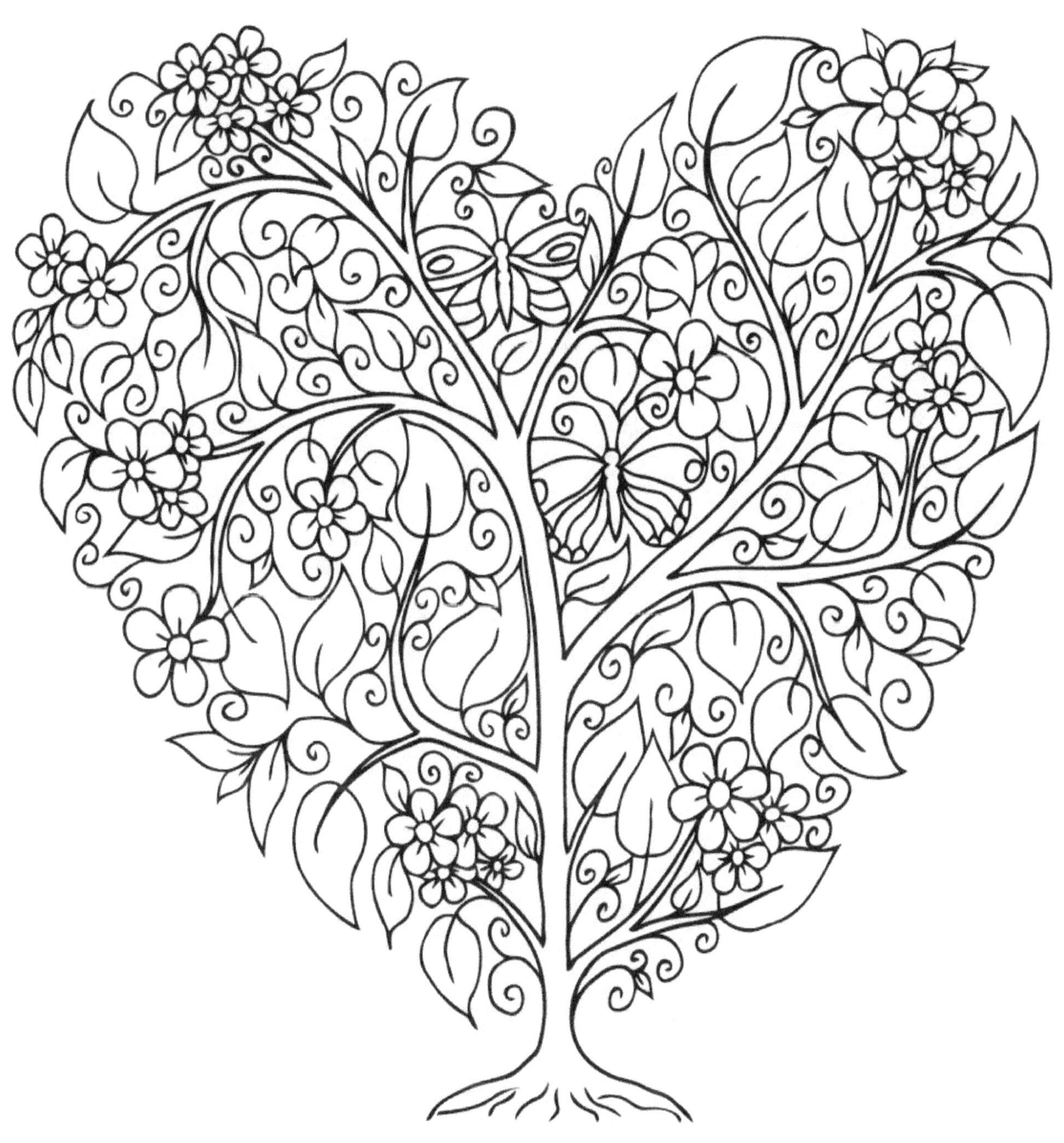

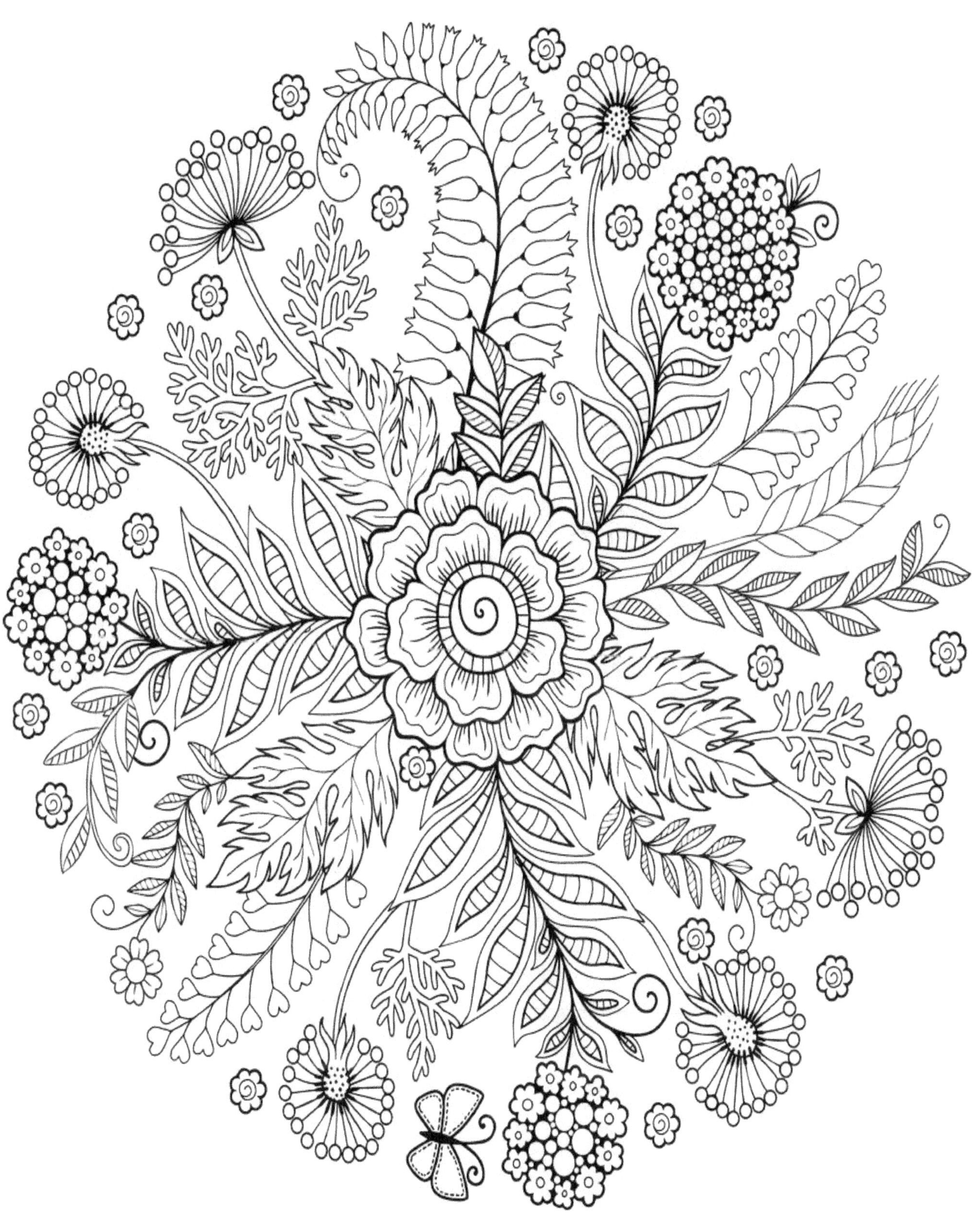

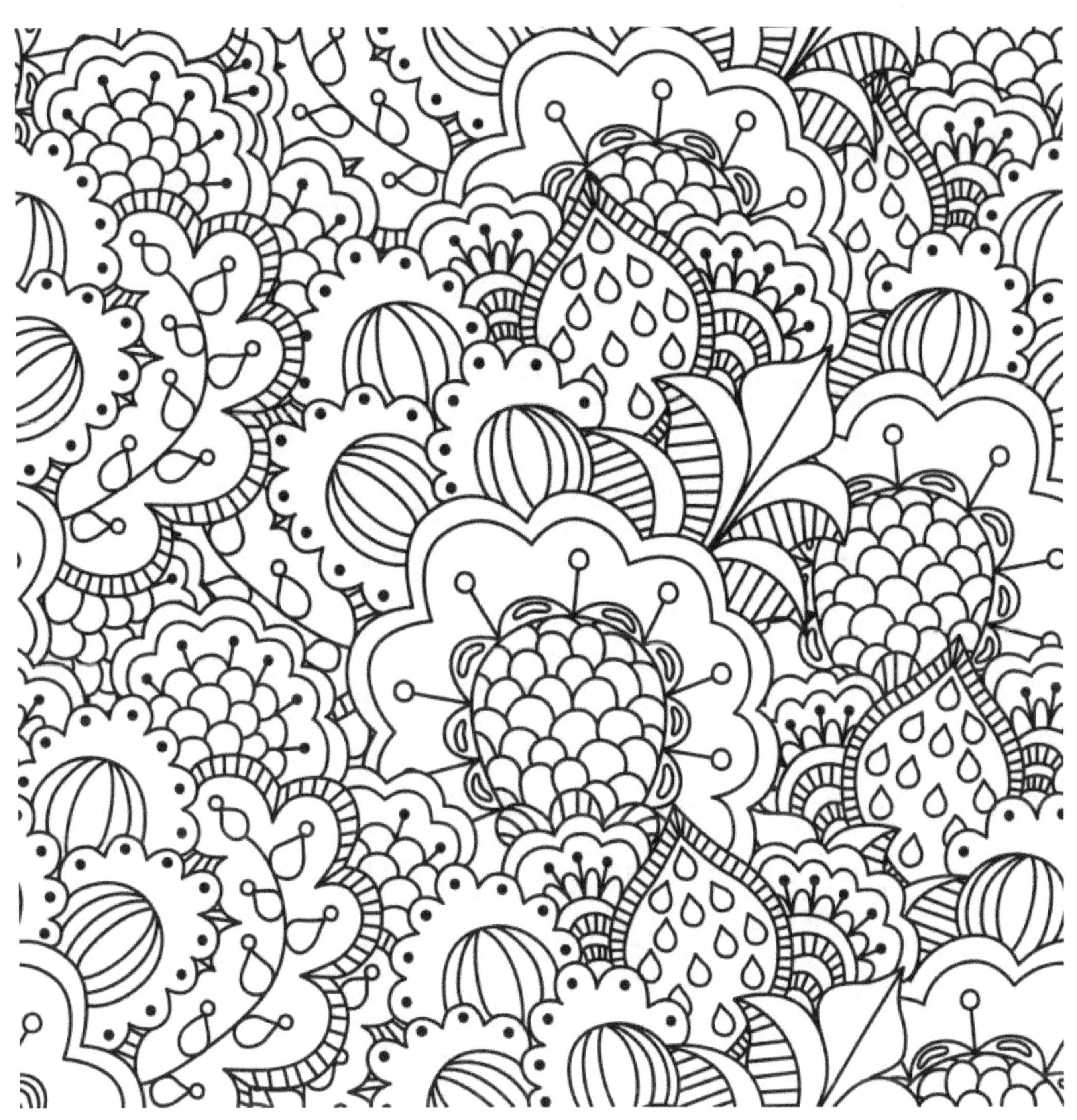

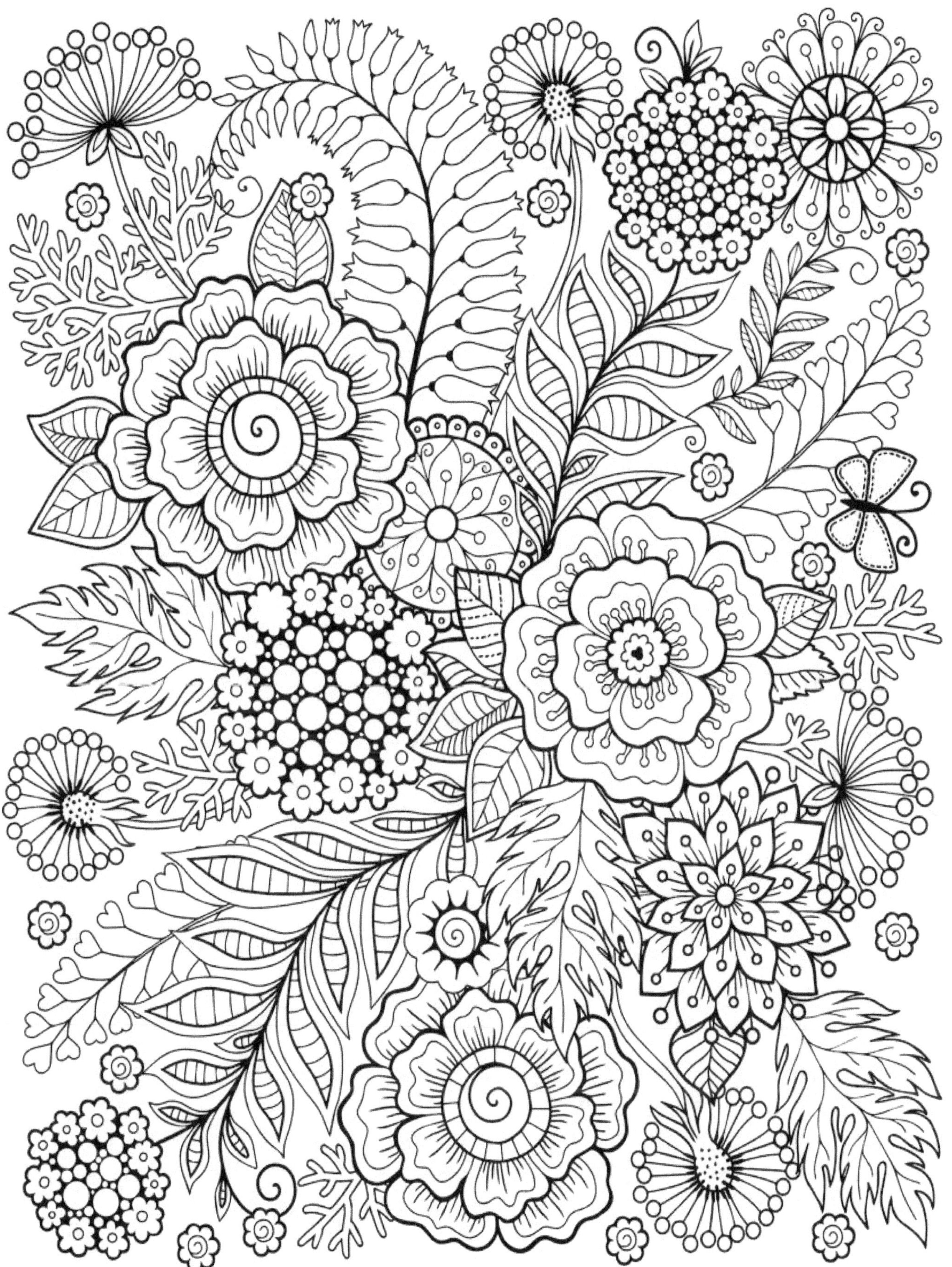

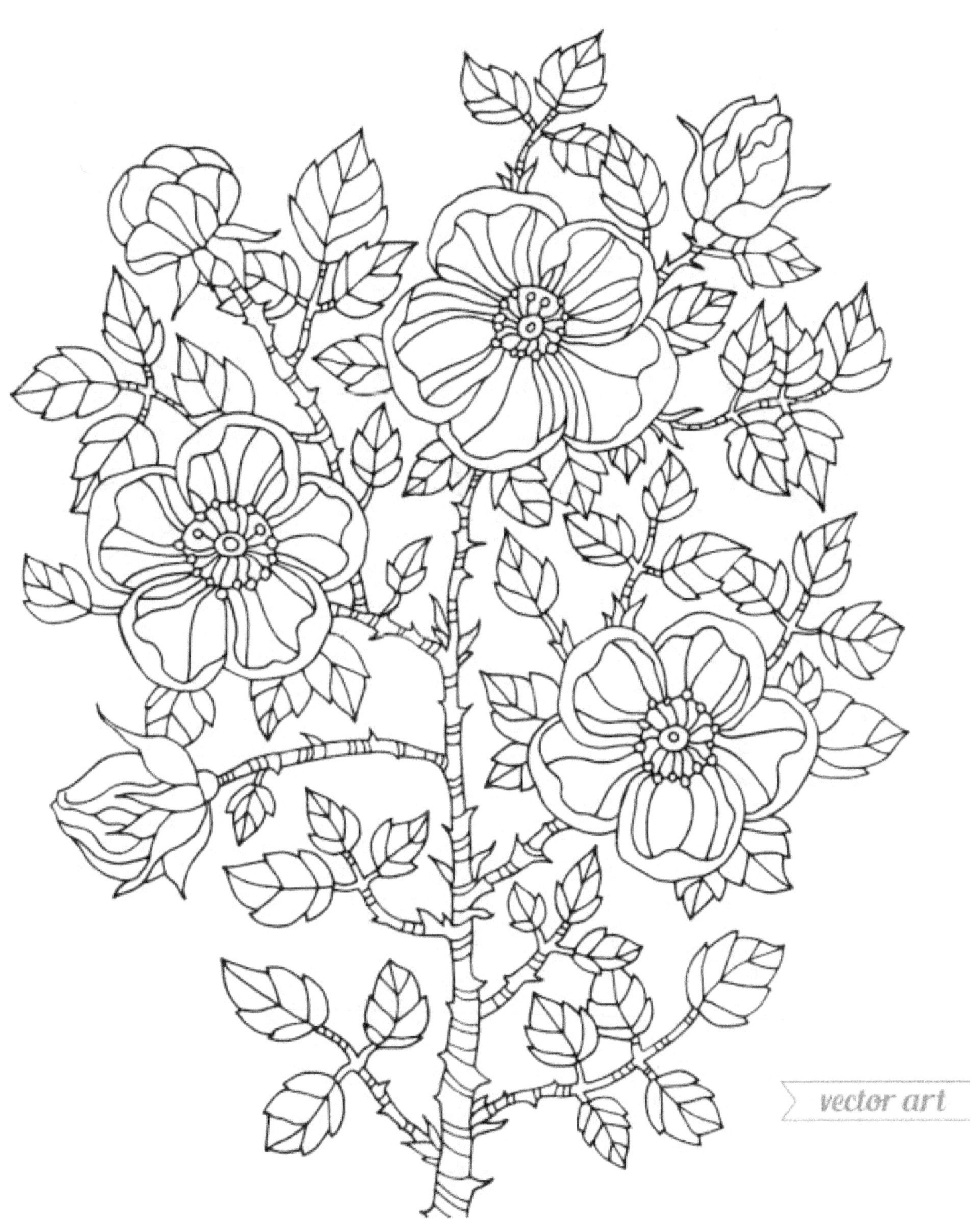

vector art

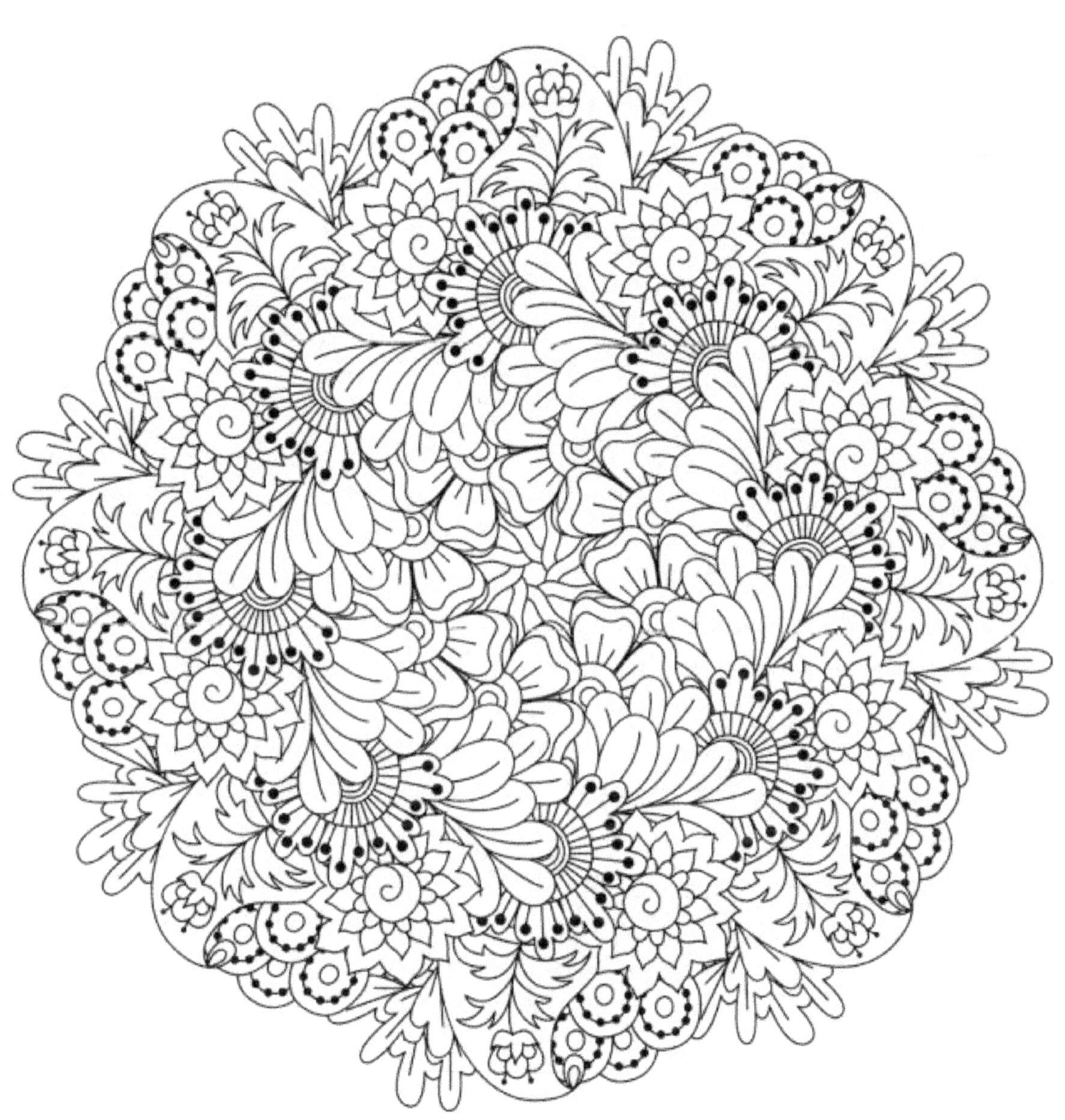

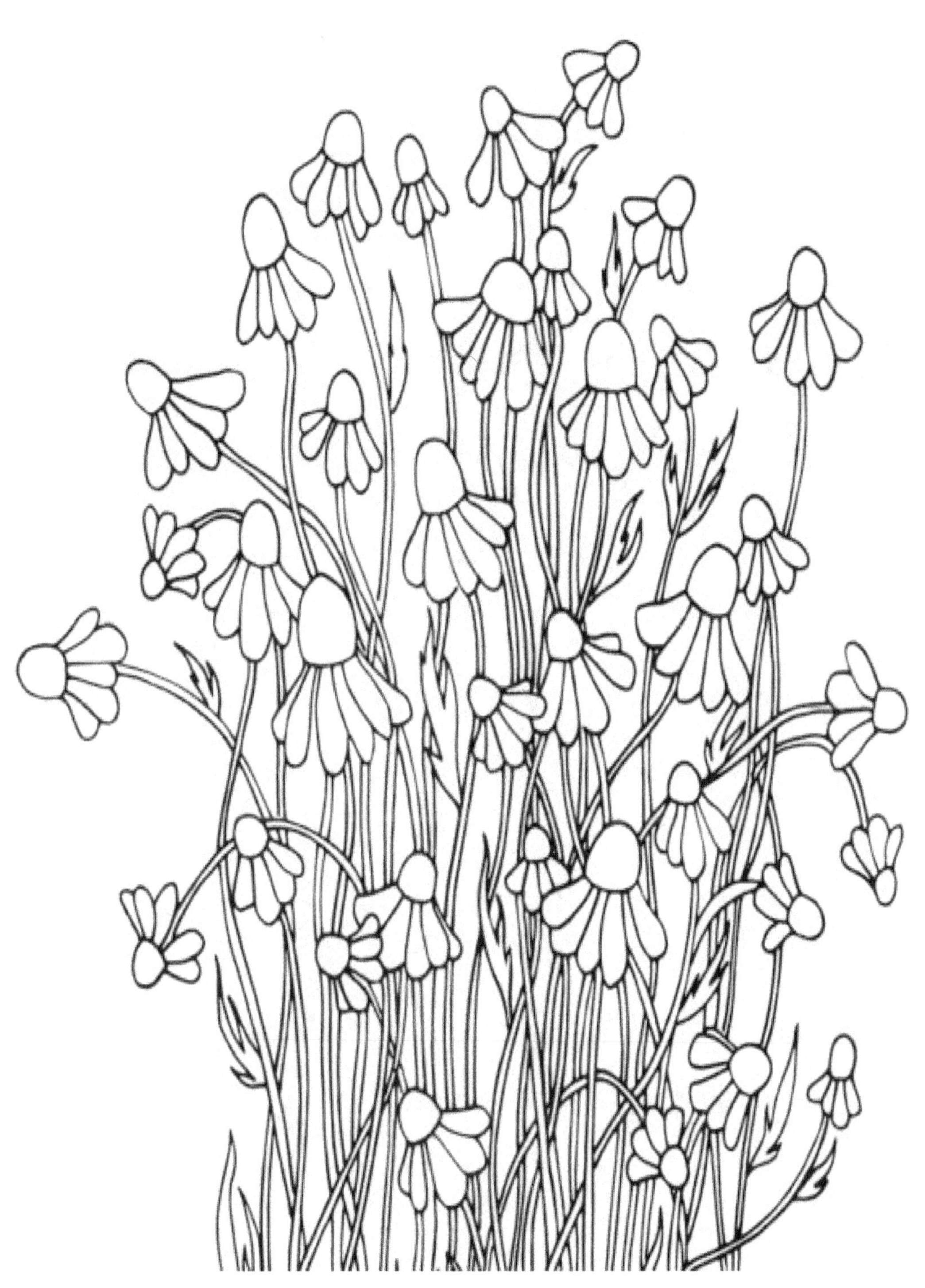

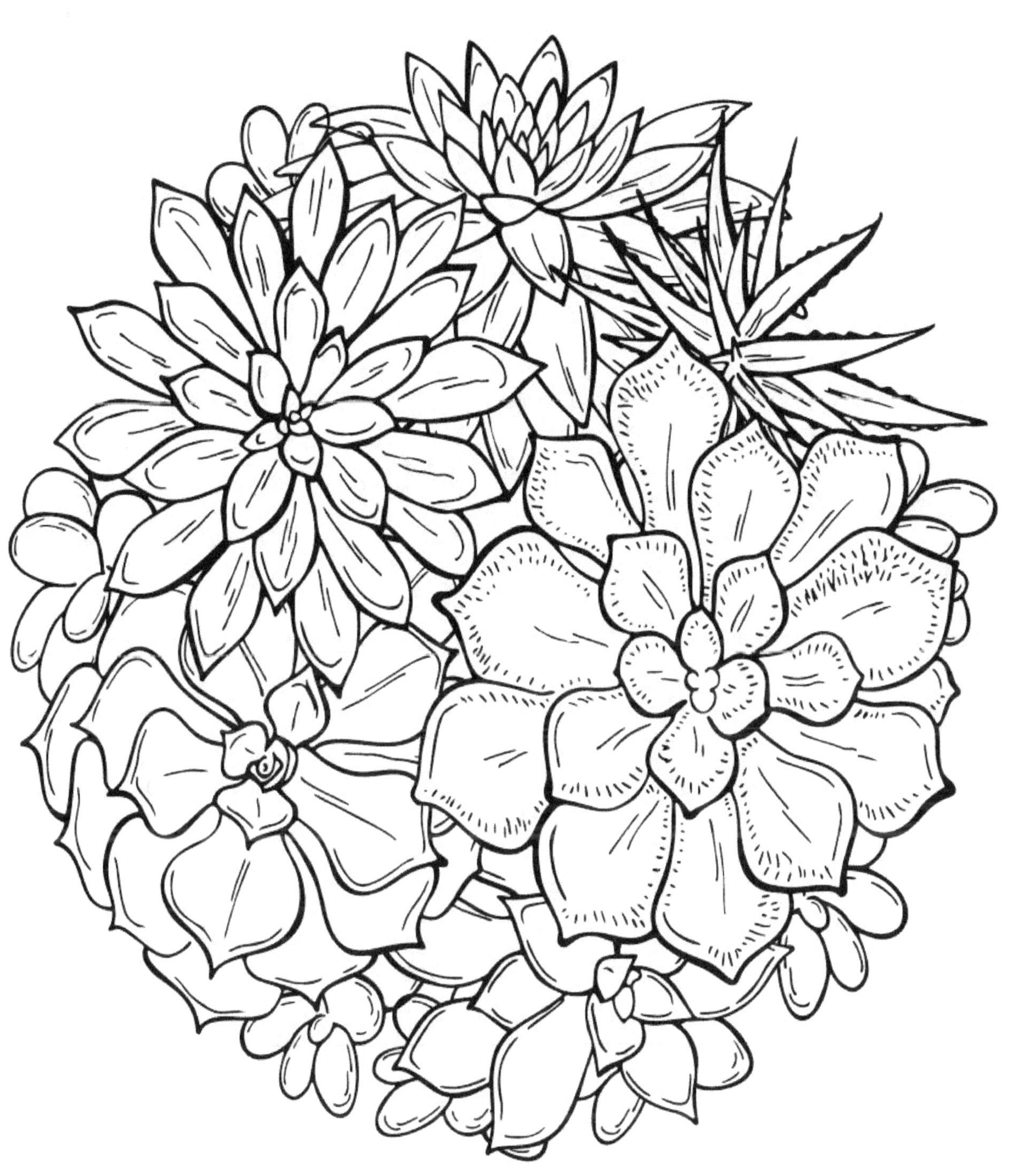

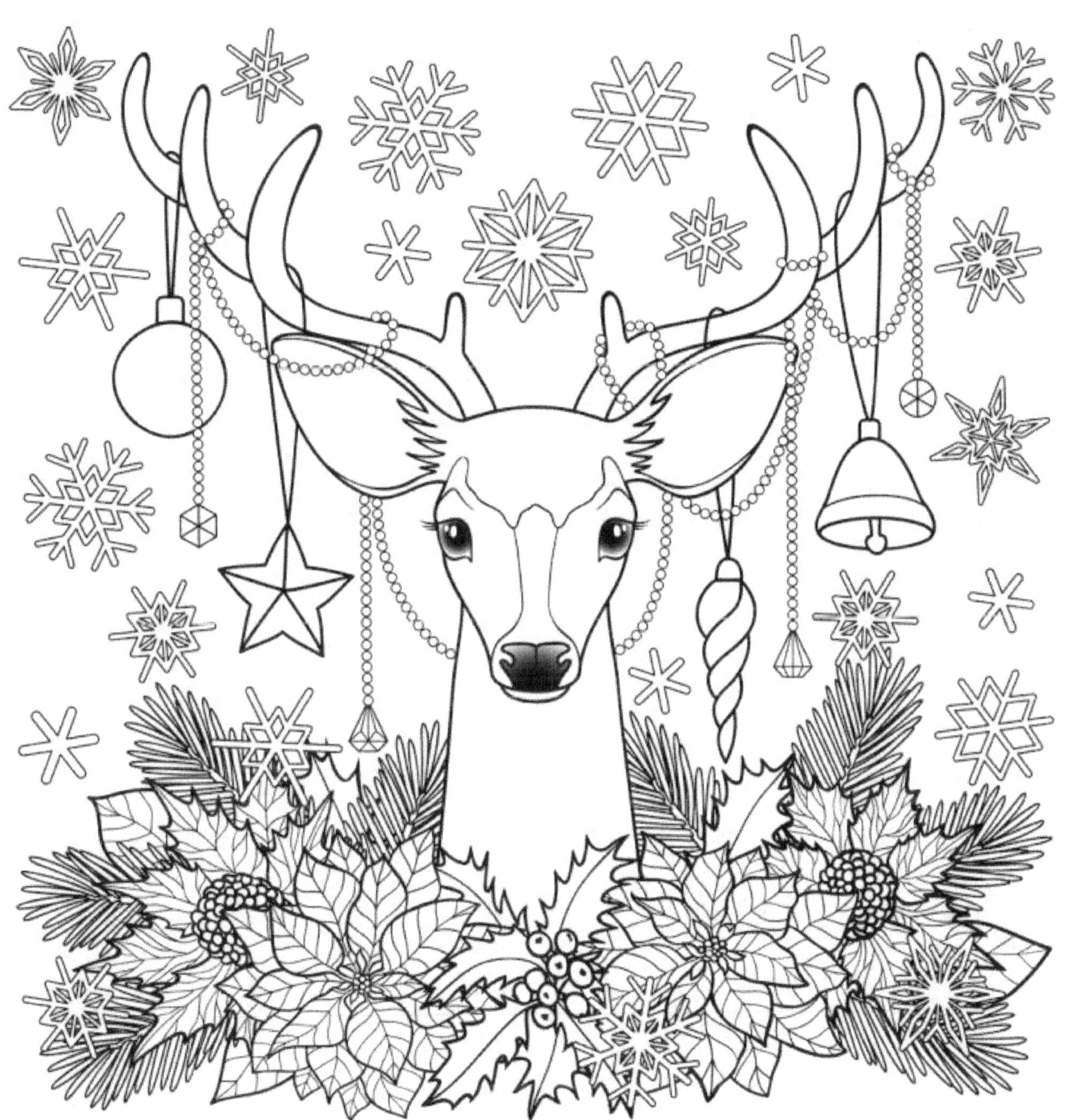

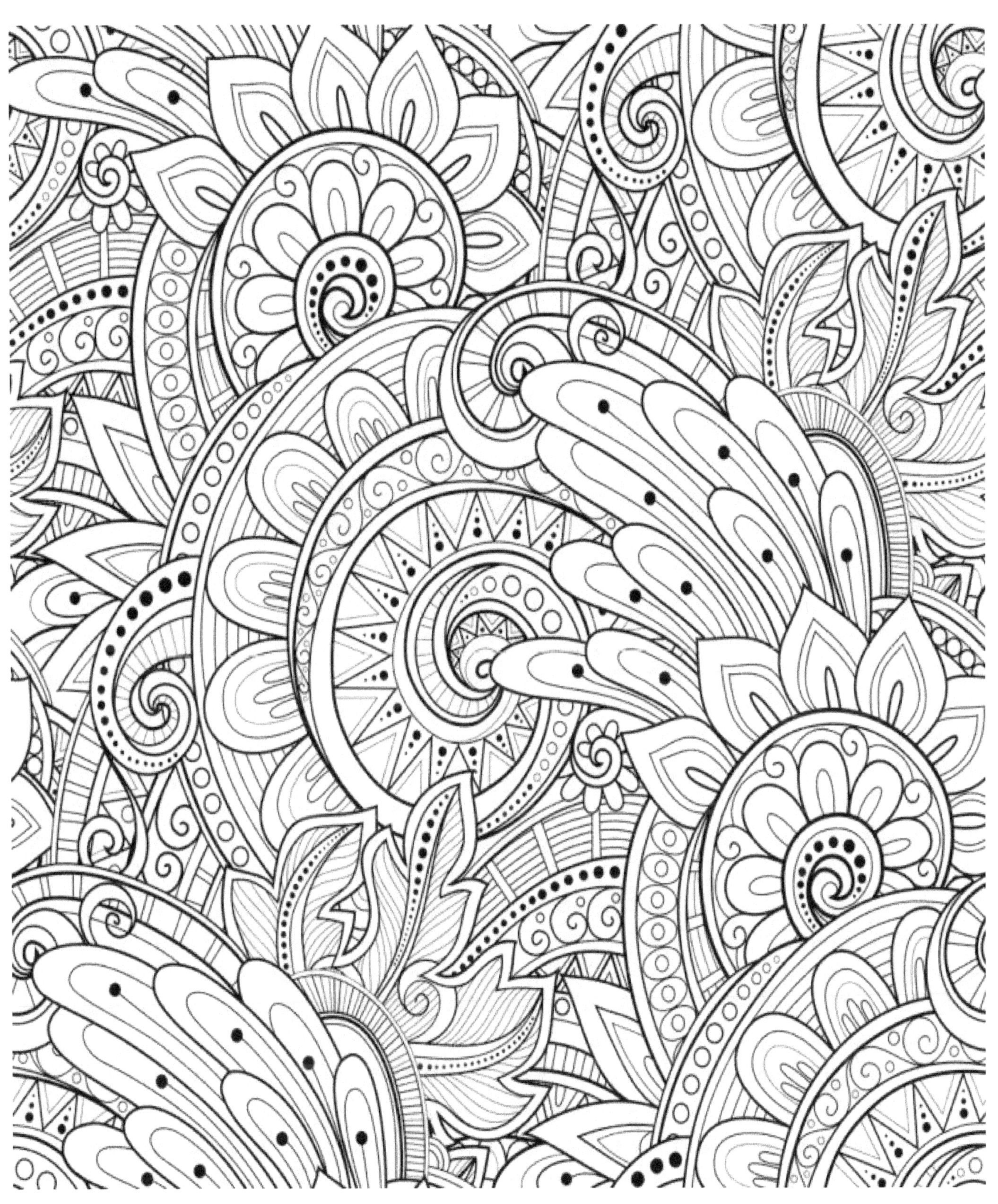

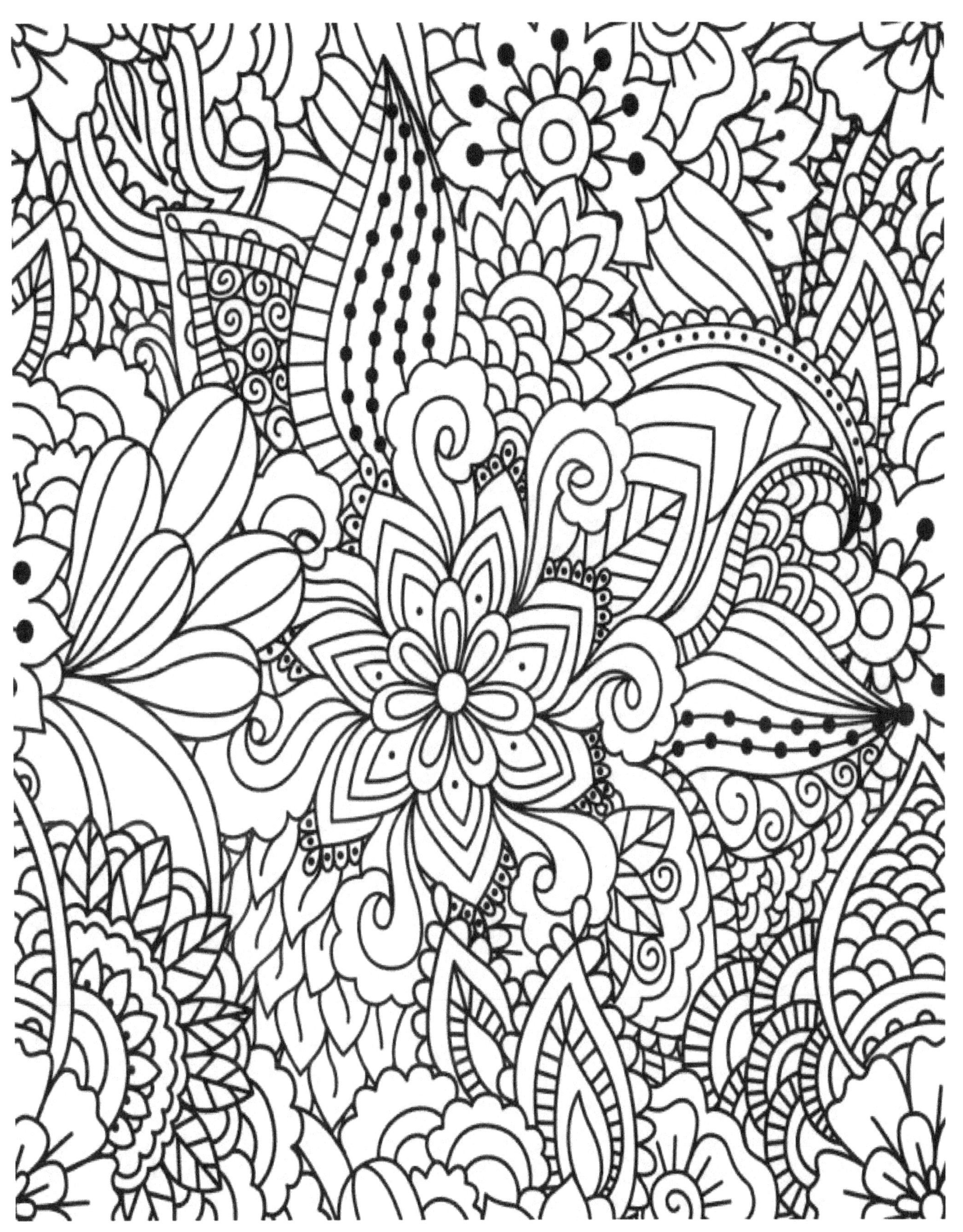

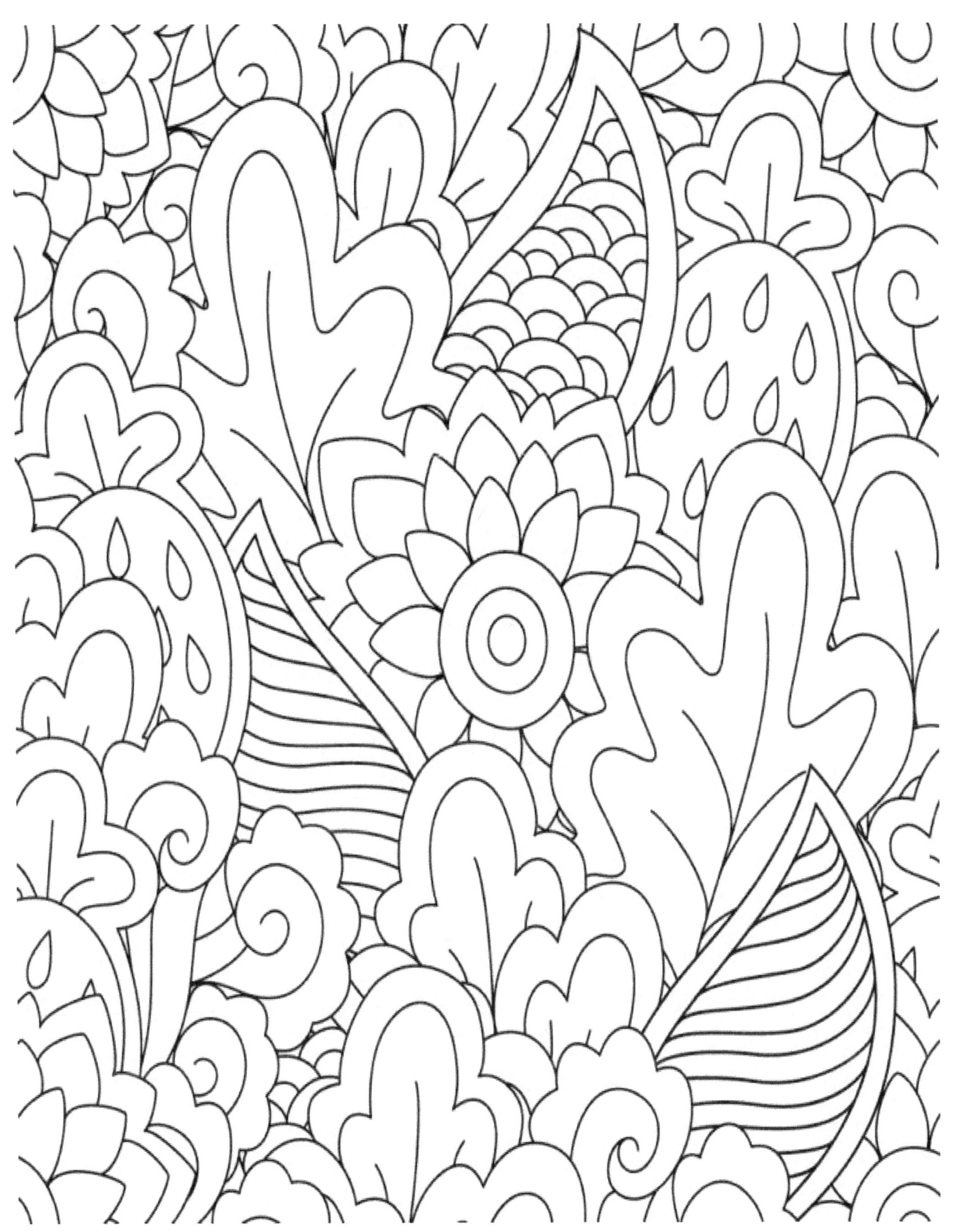

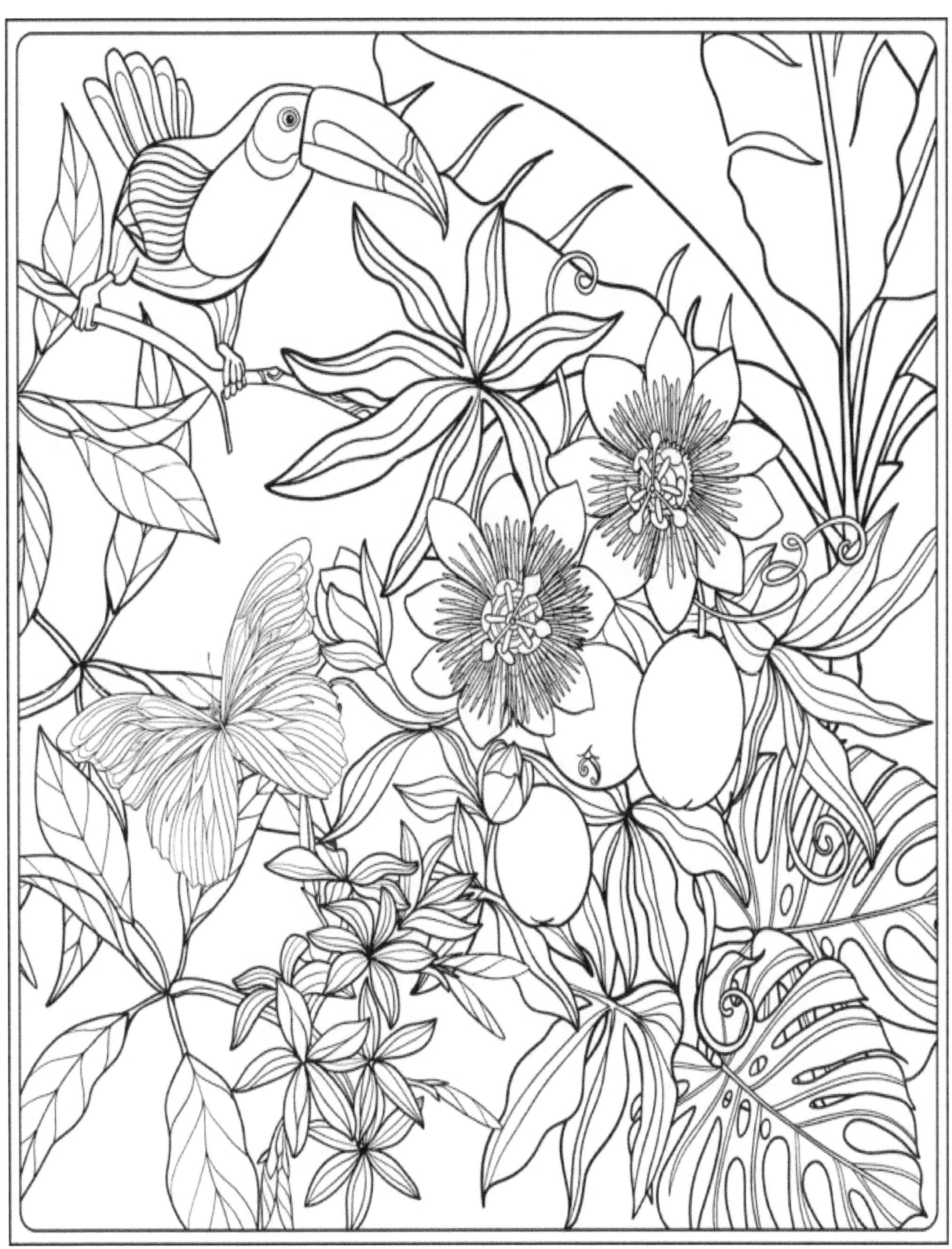

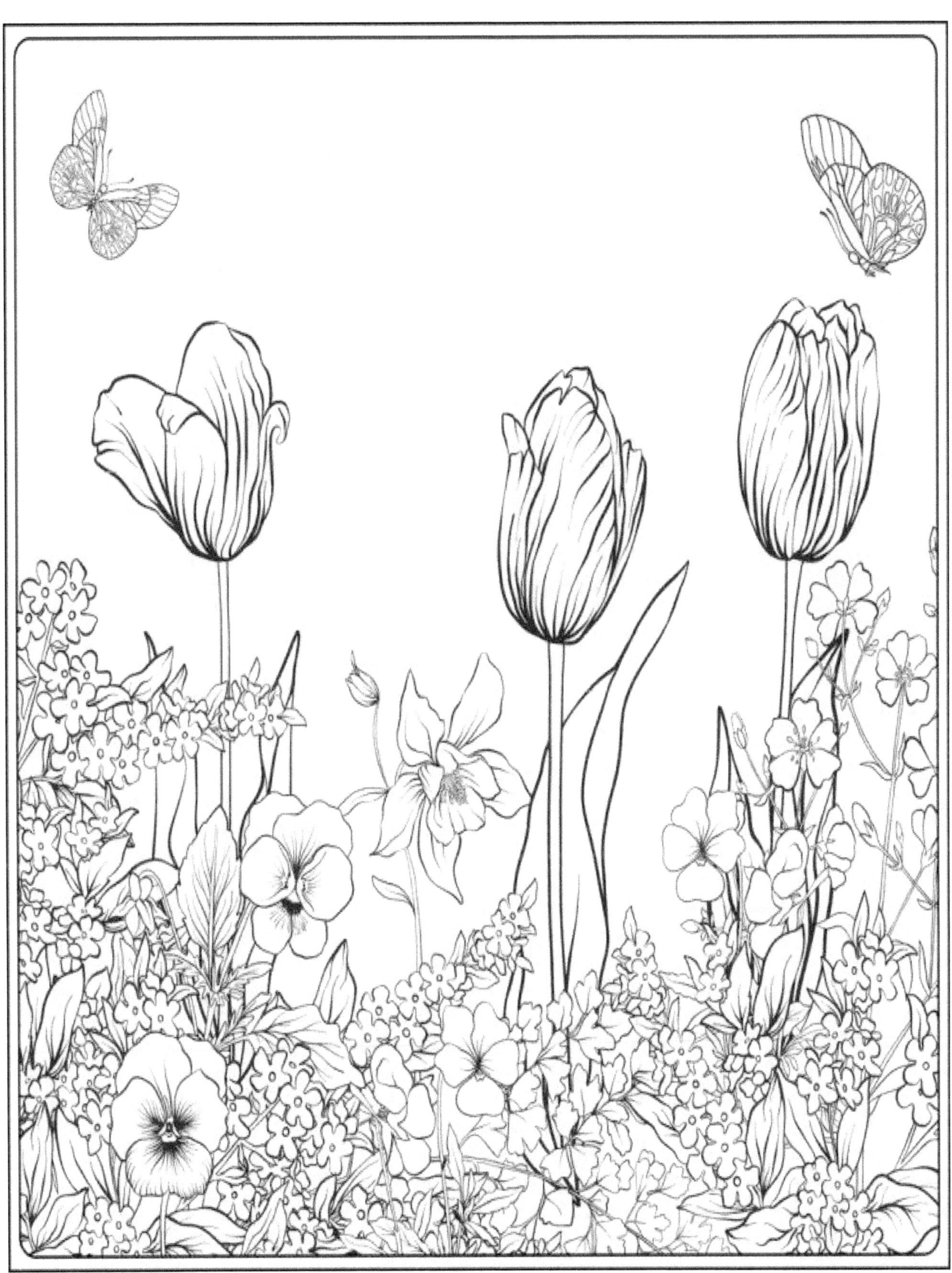

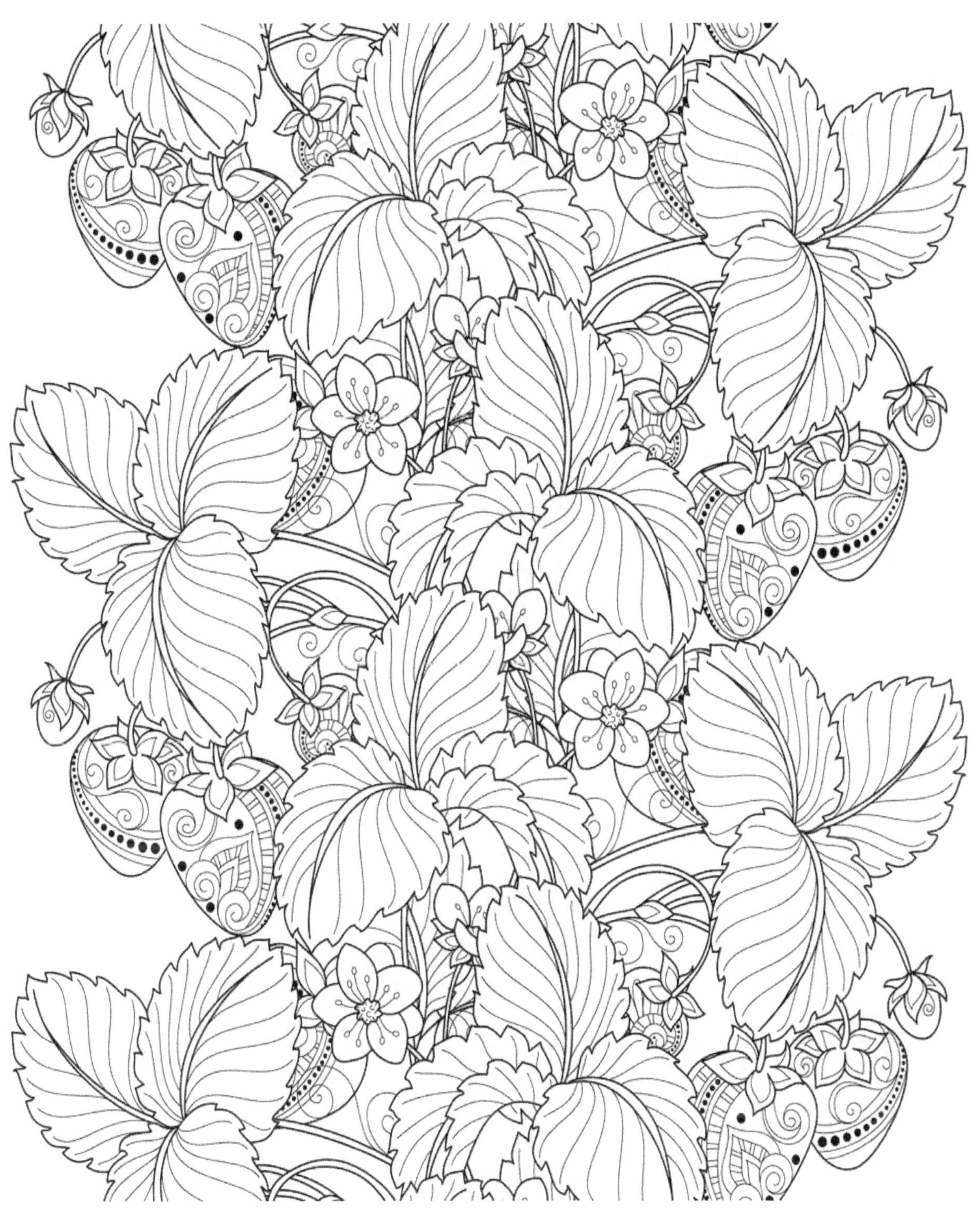

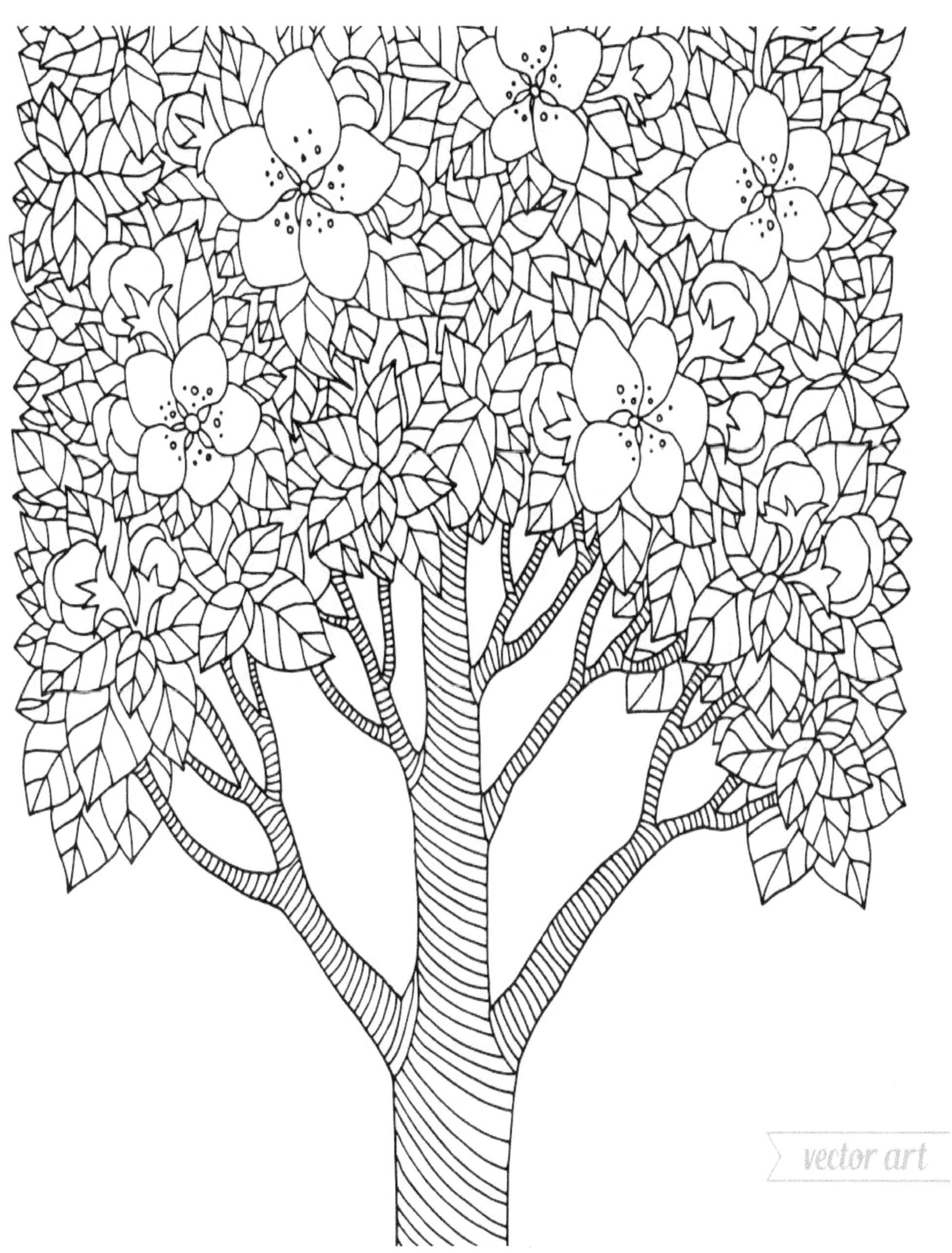

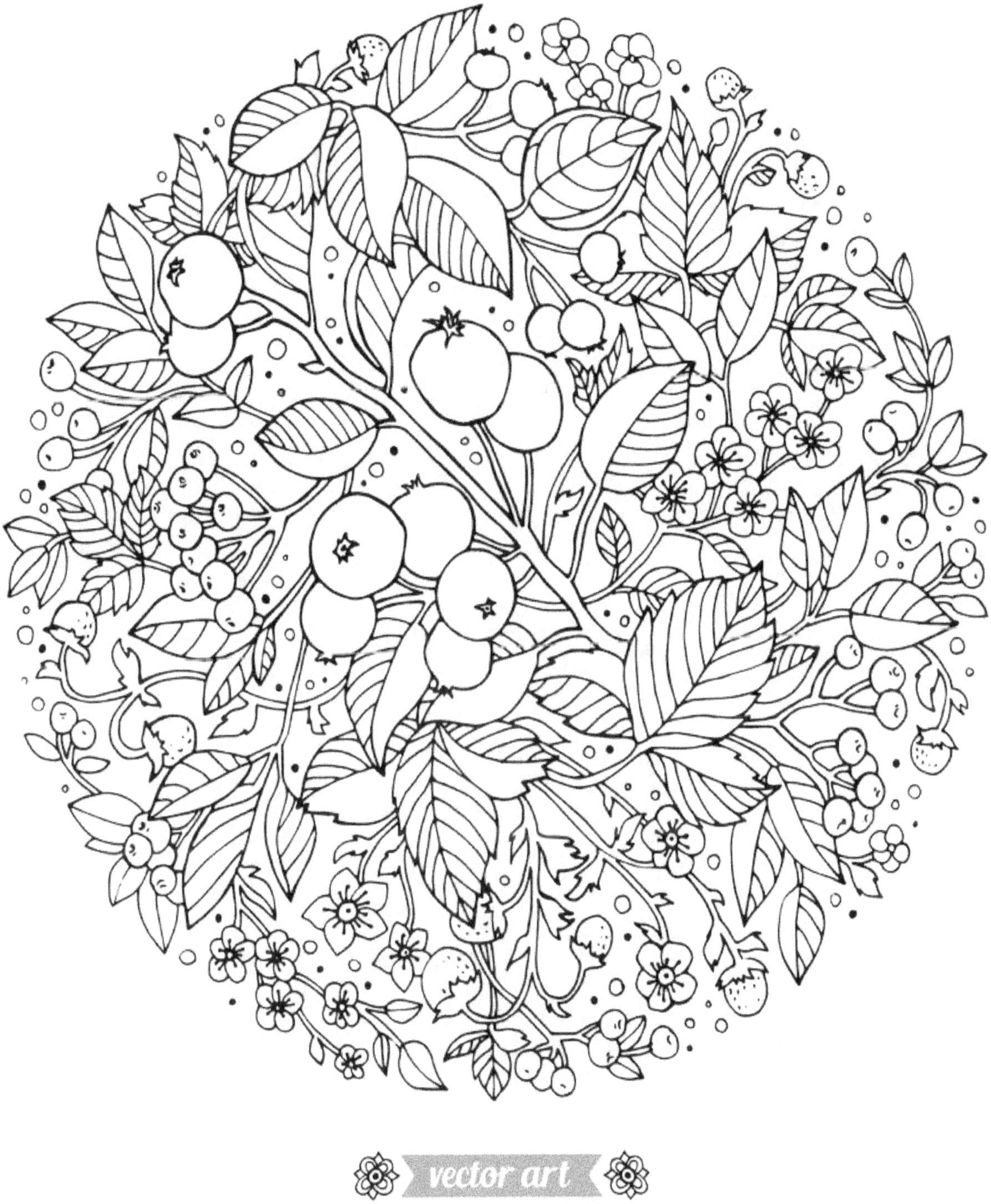

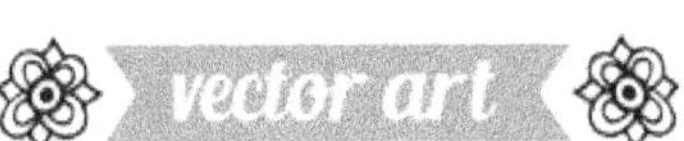
vector art

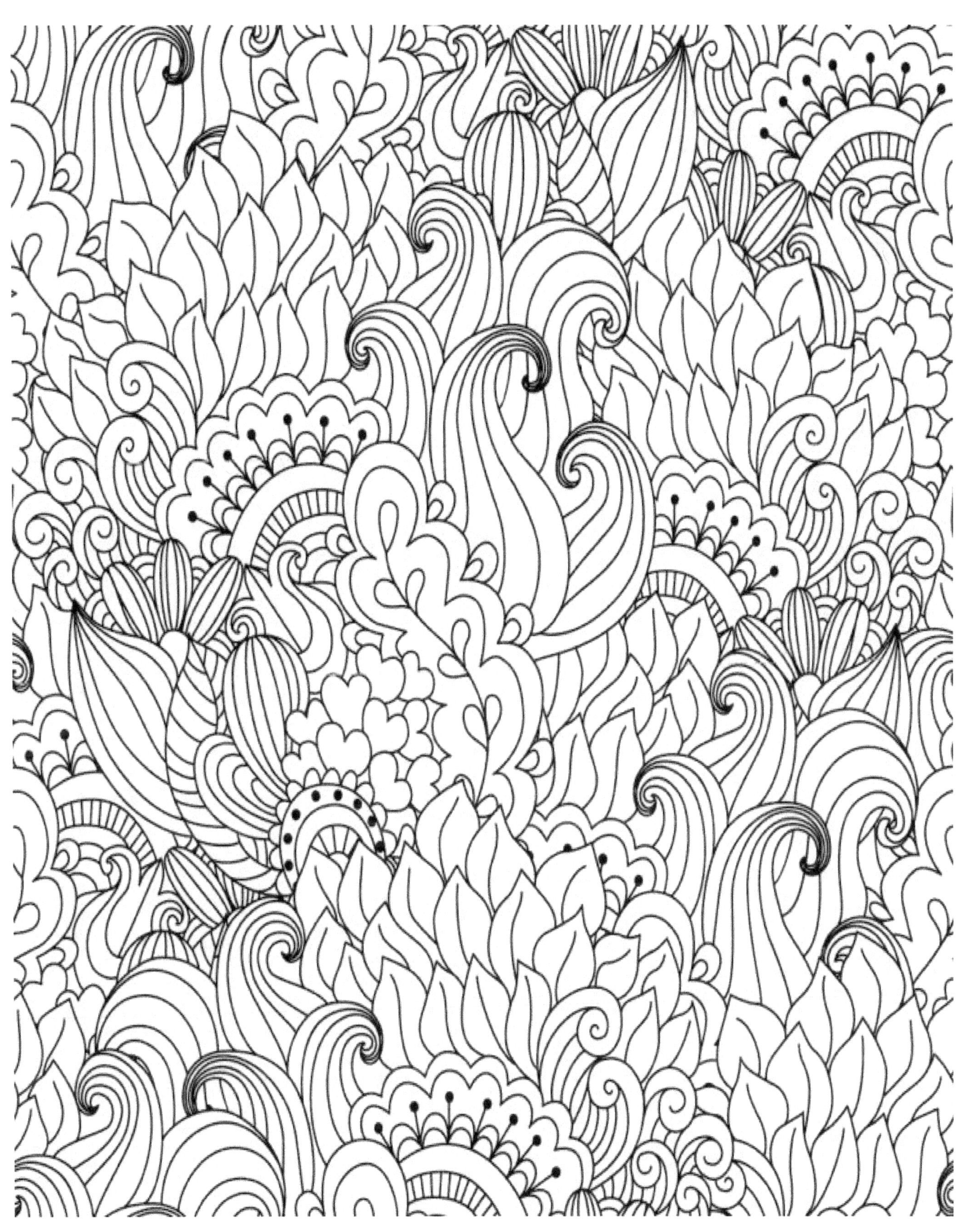

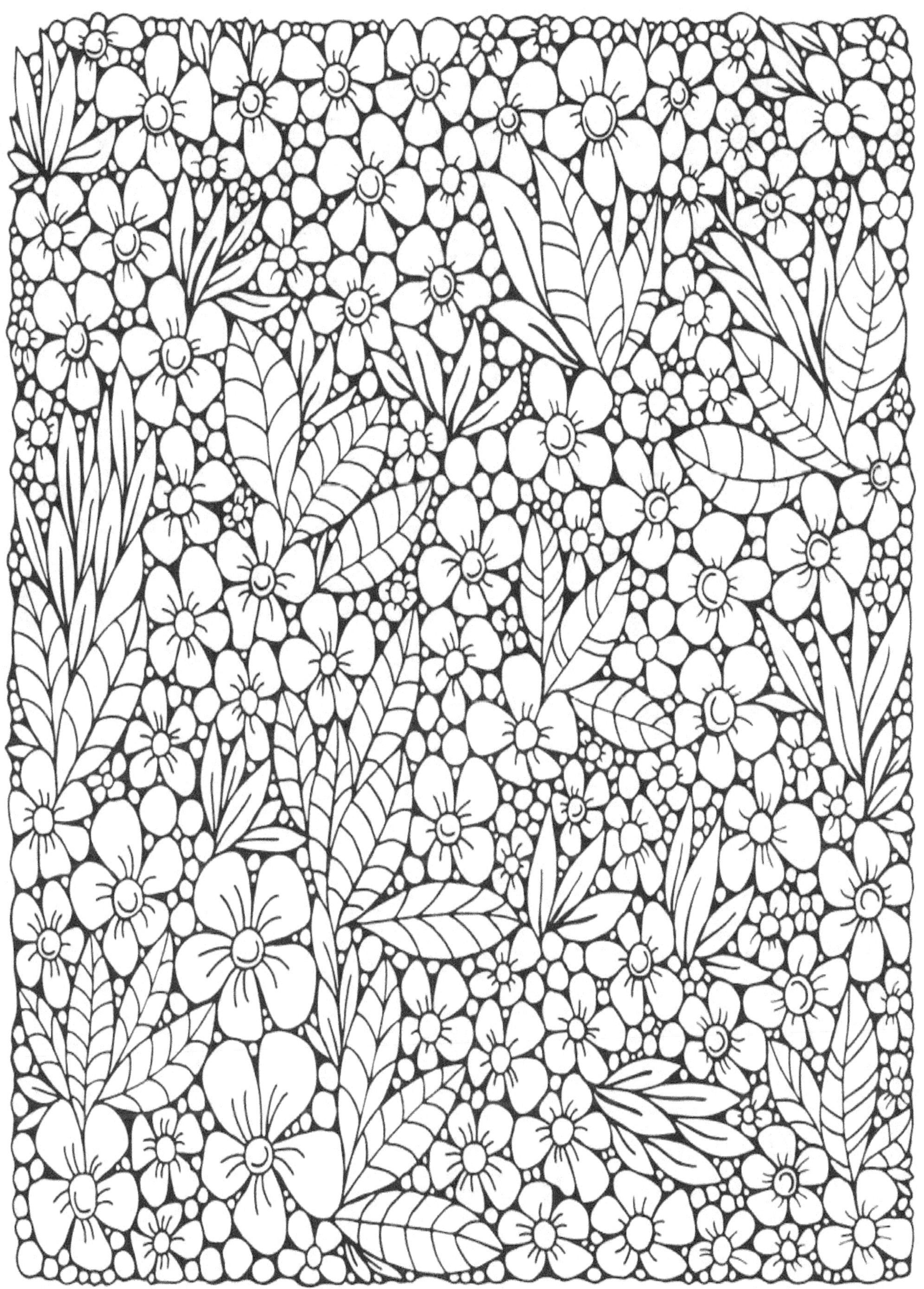

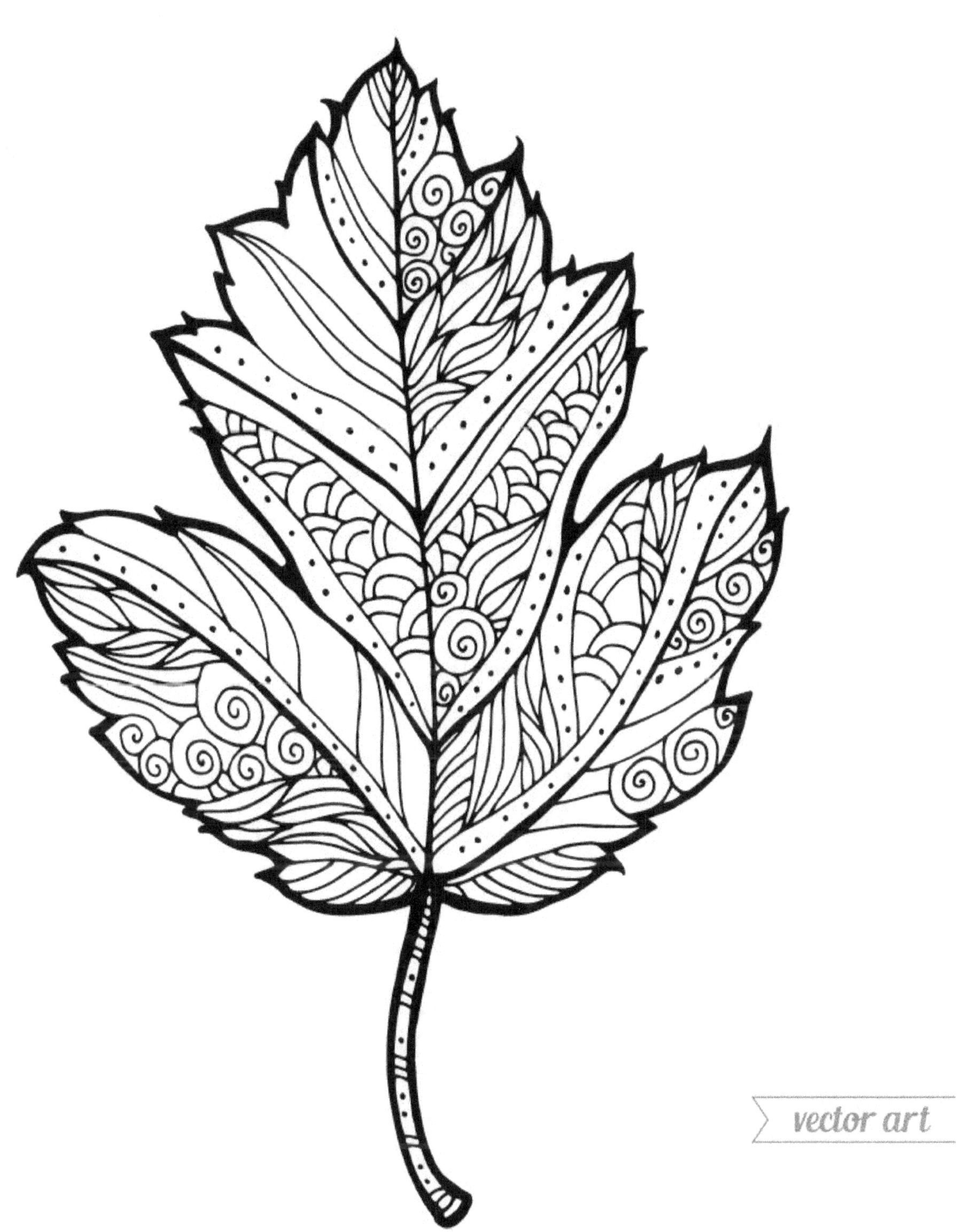

vector art

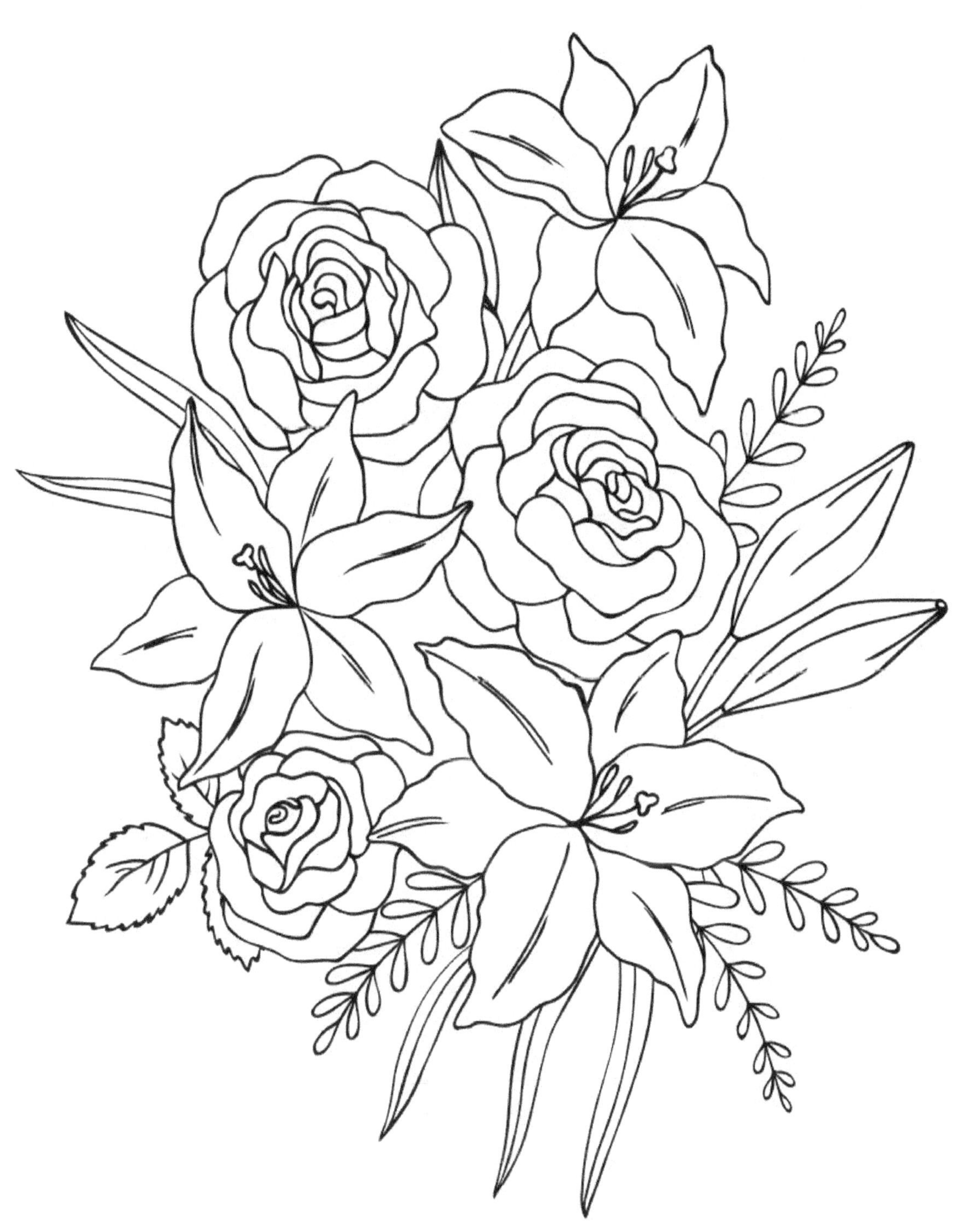

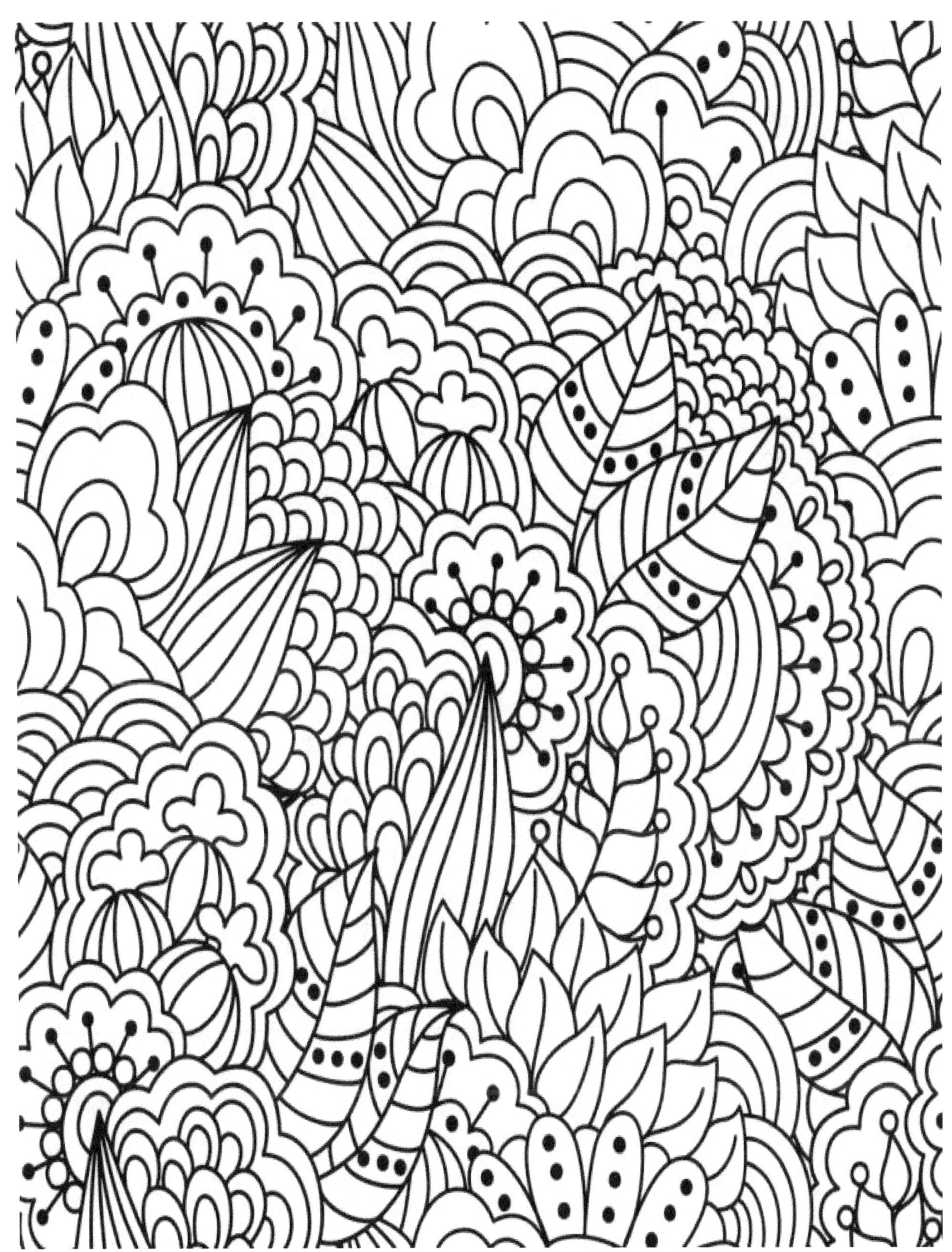

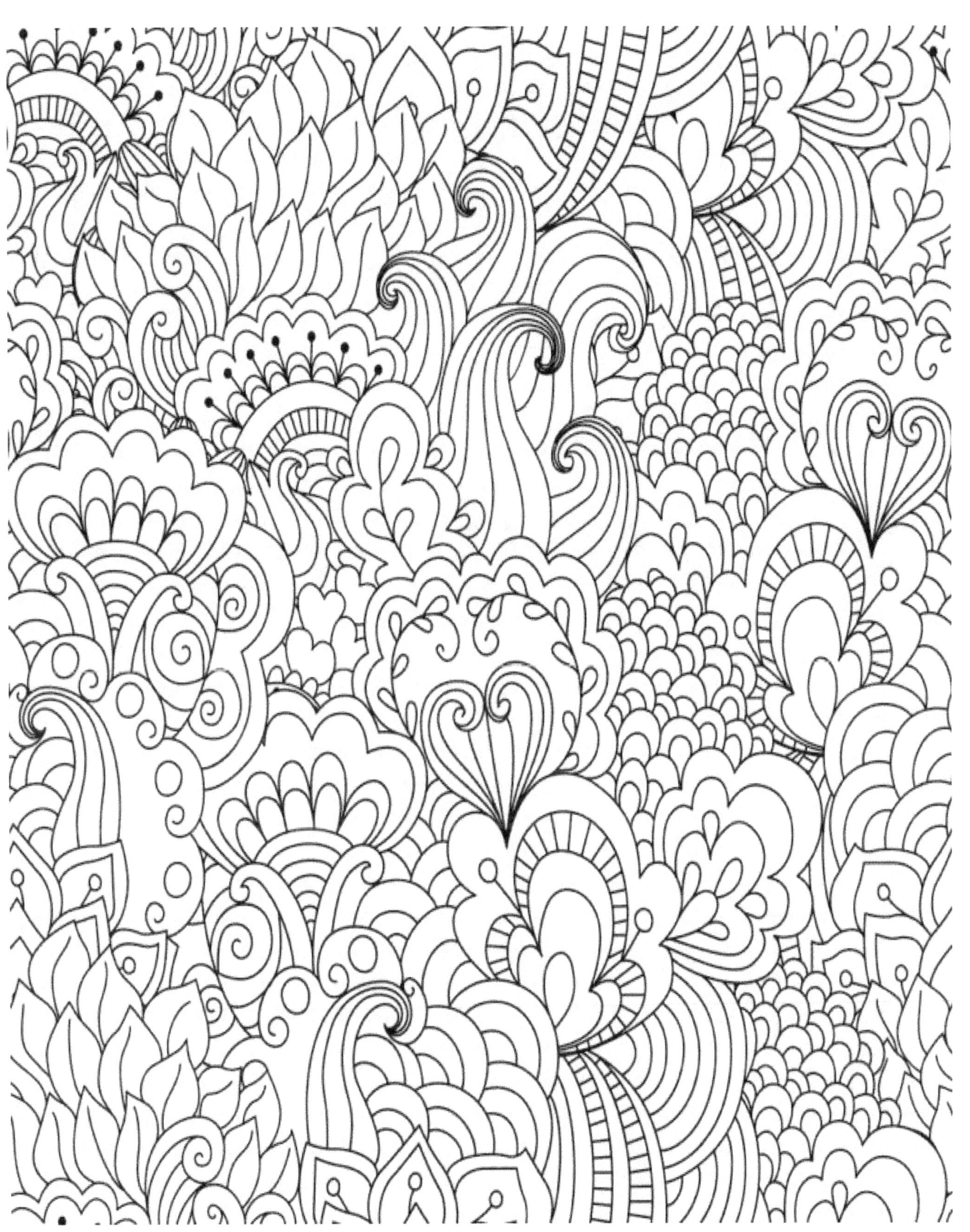

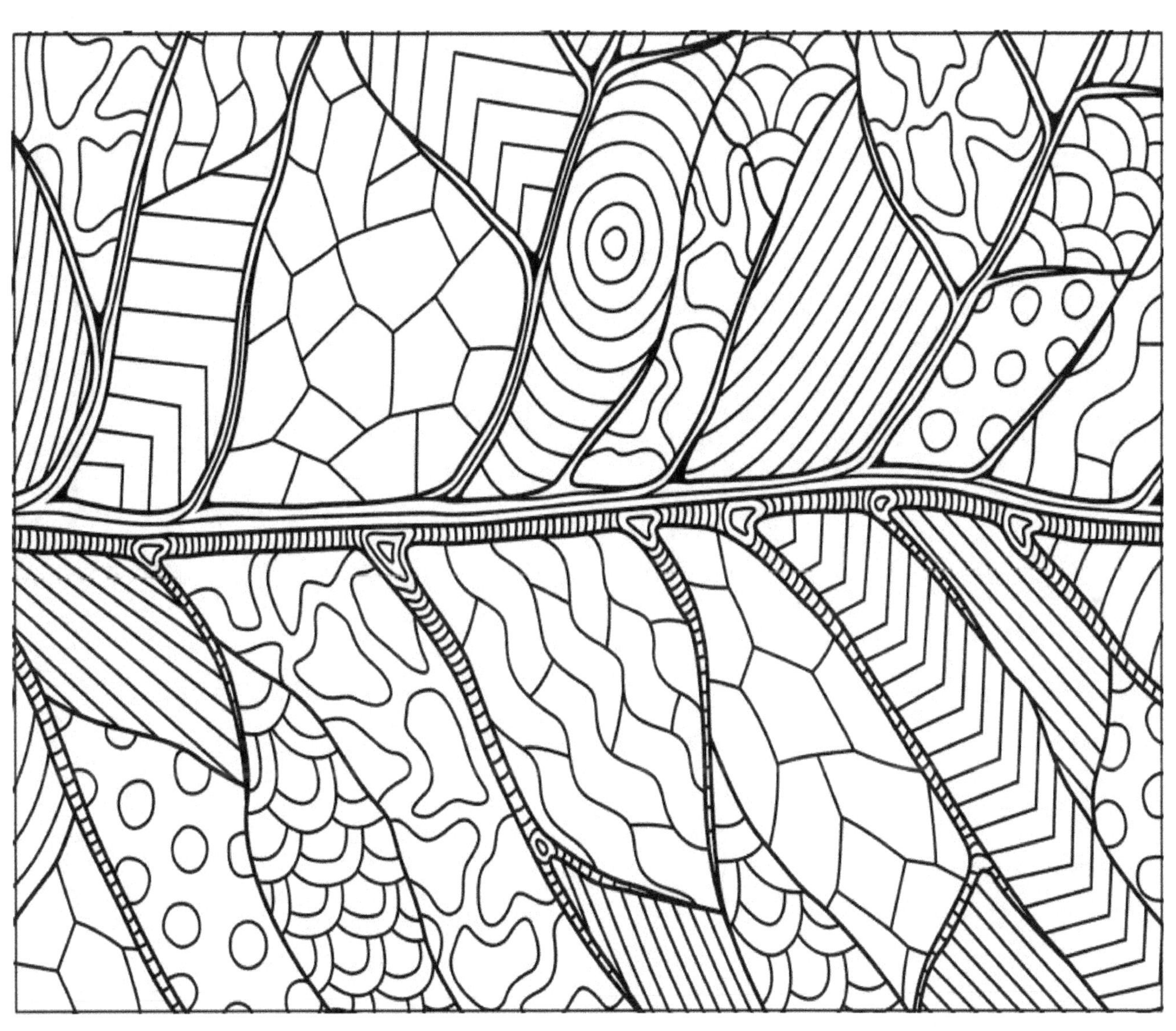

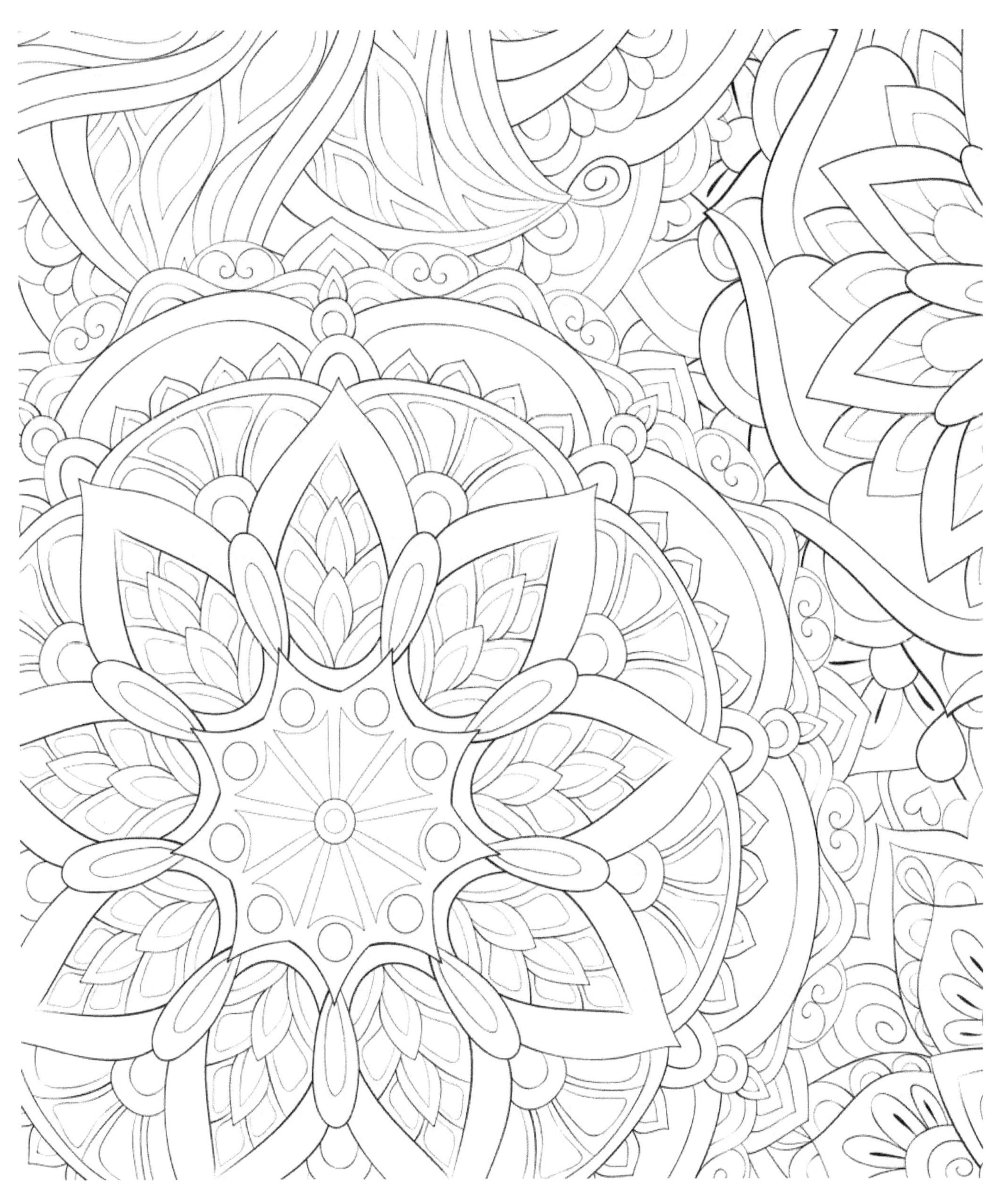

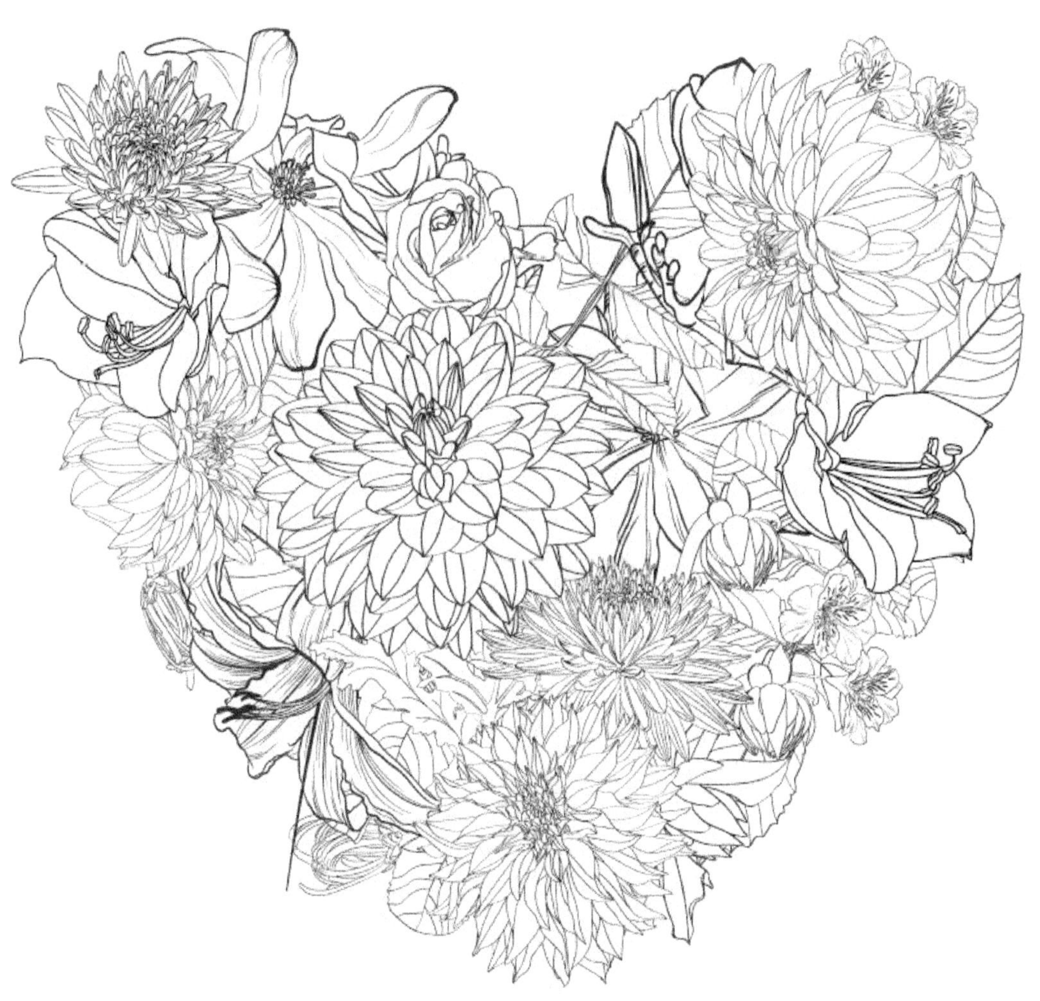

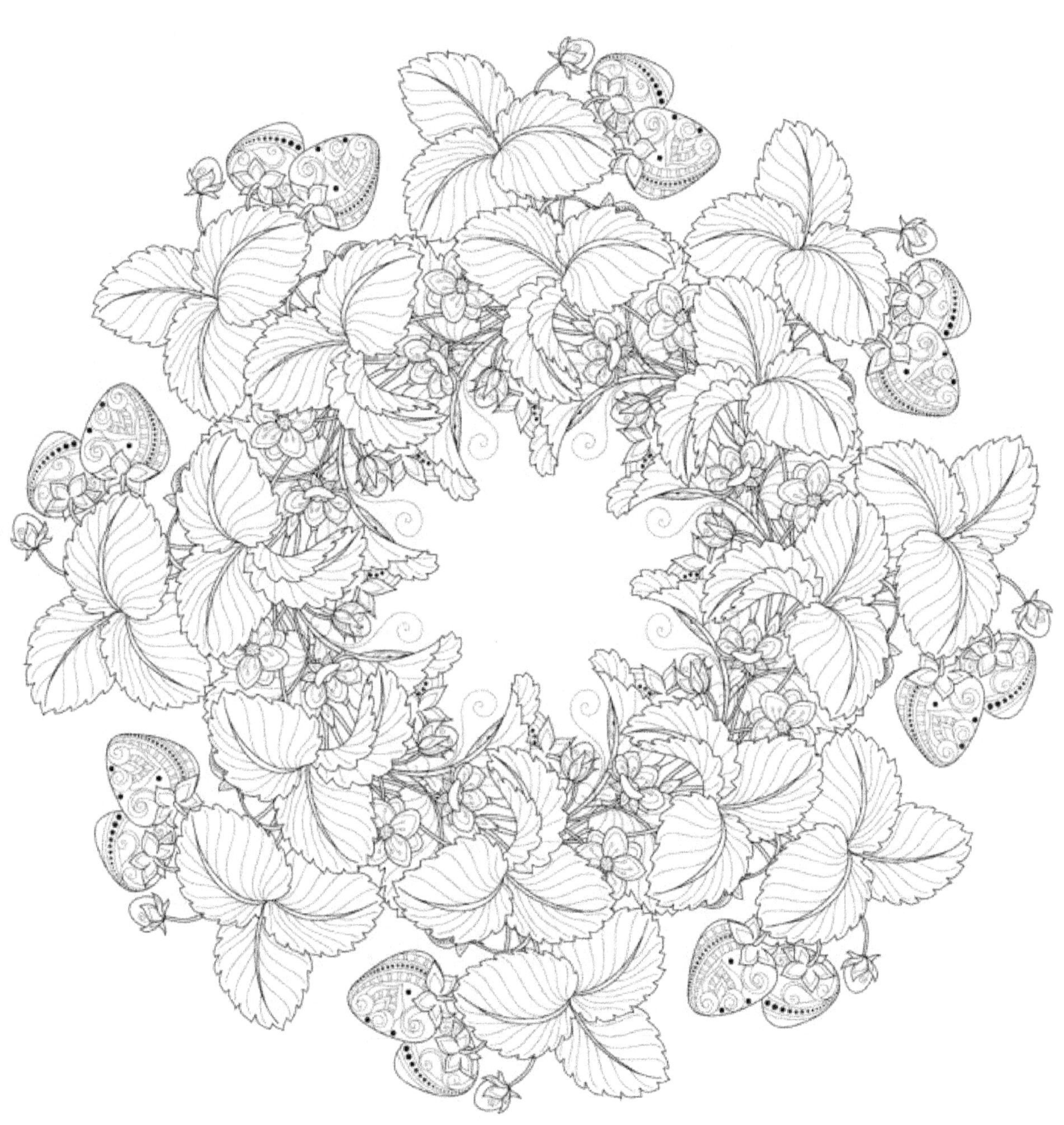

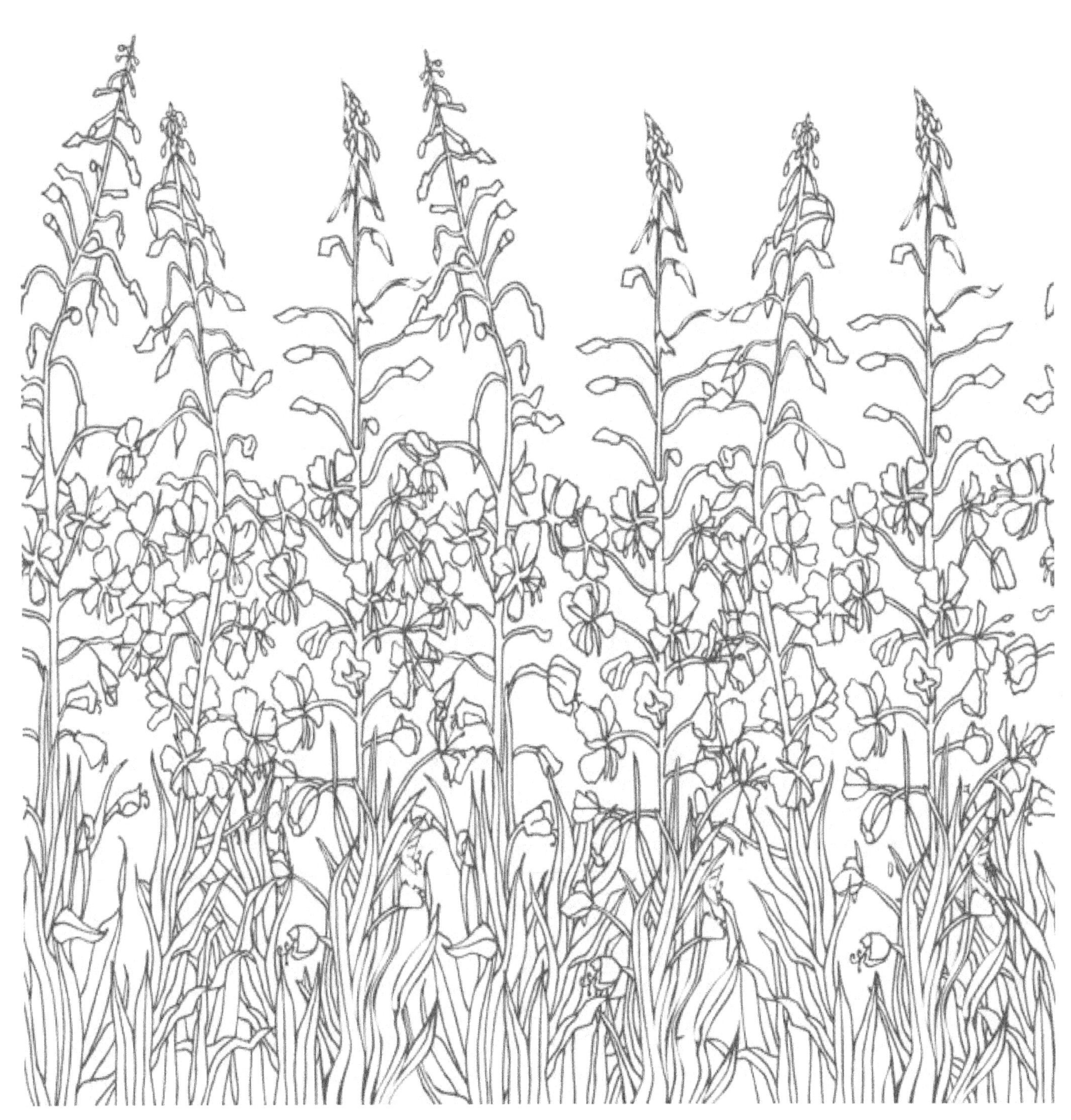

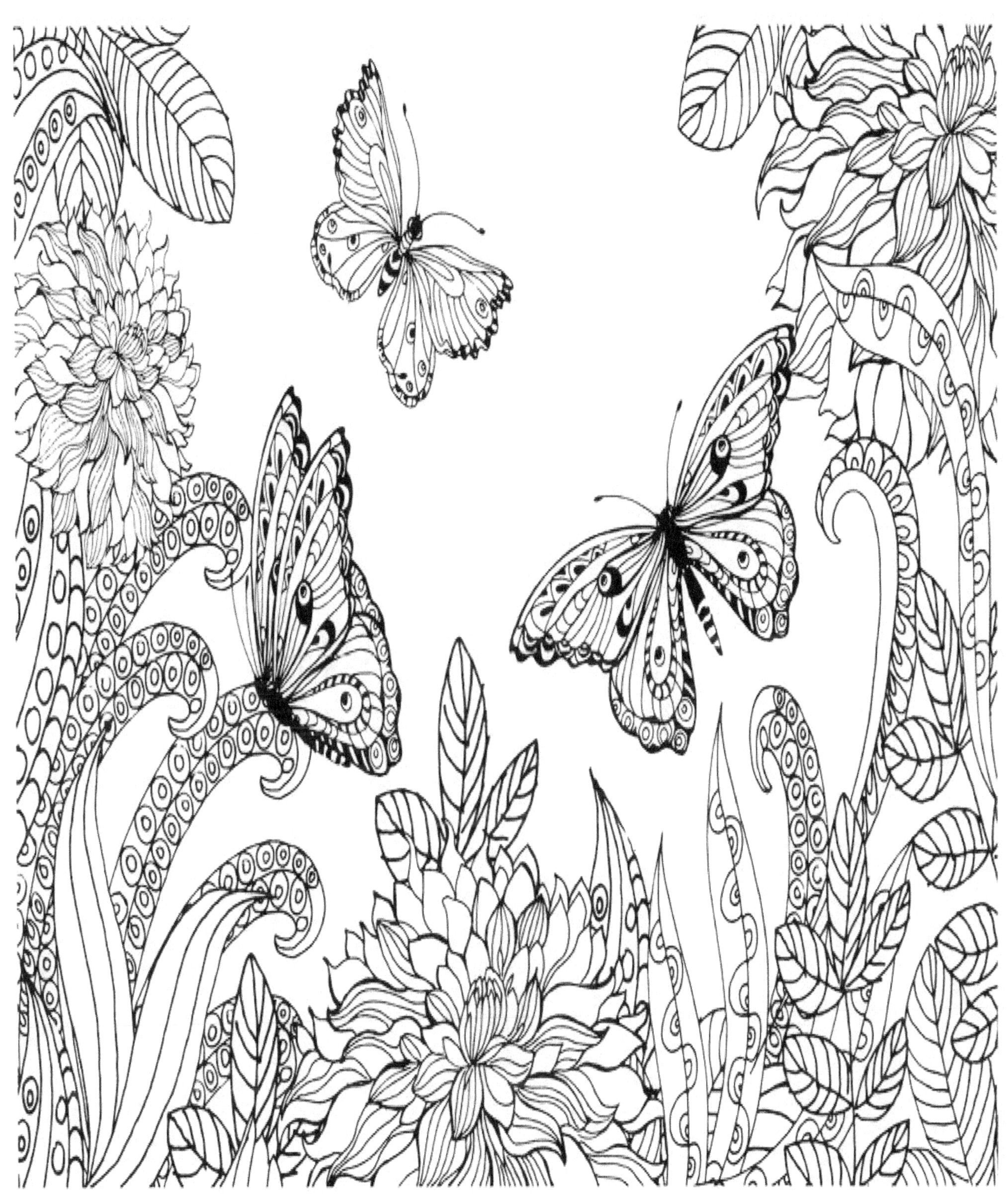

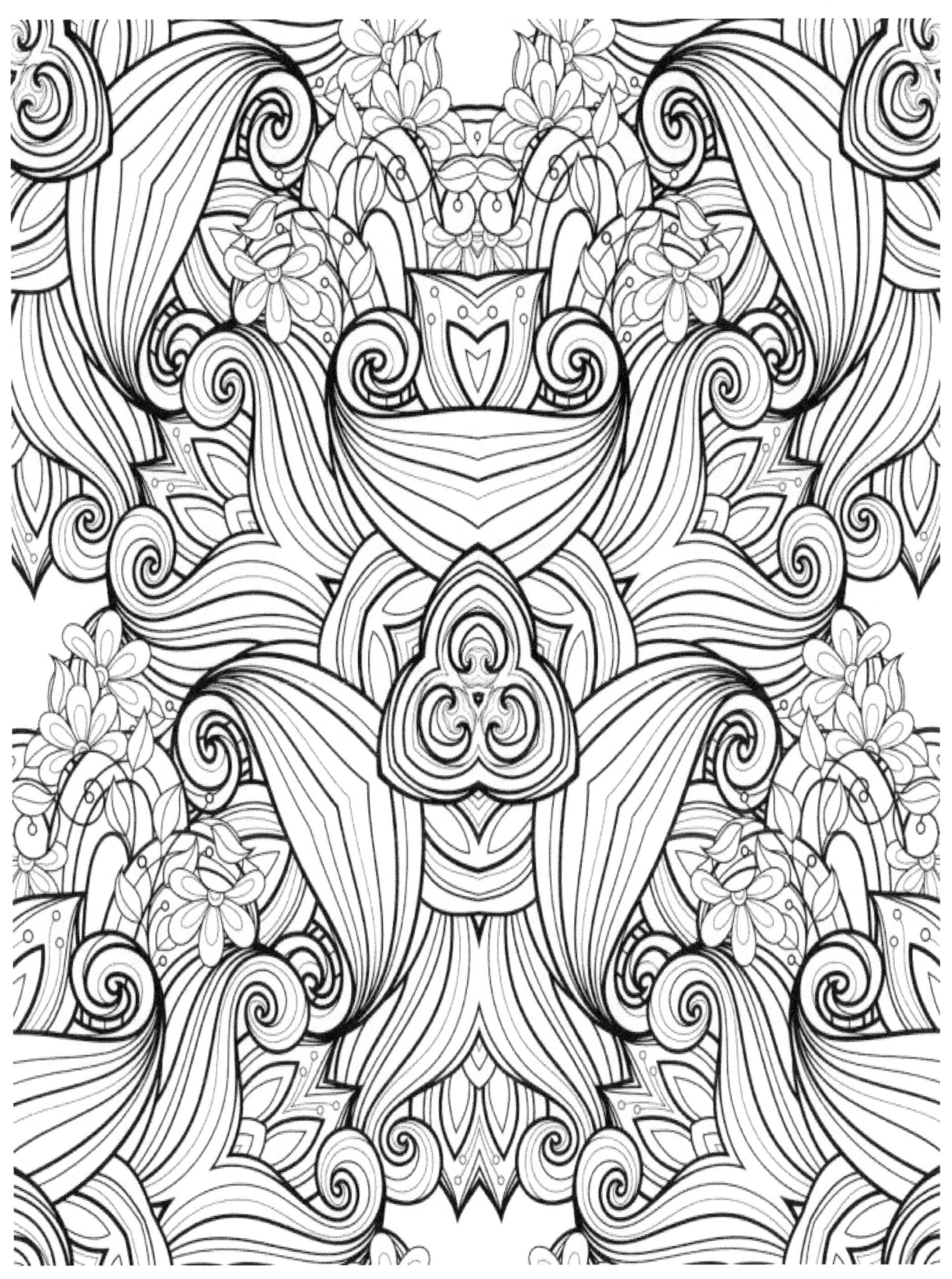

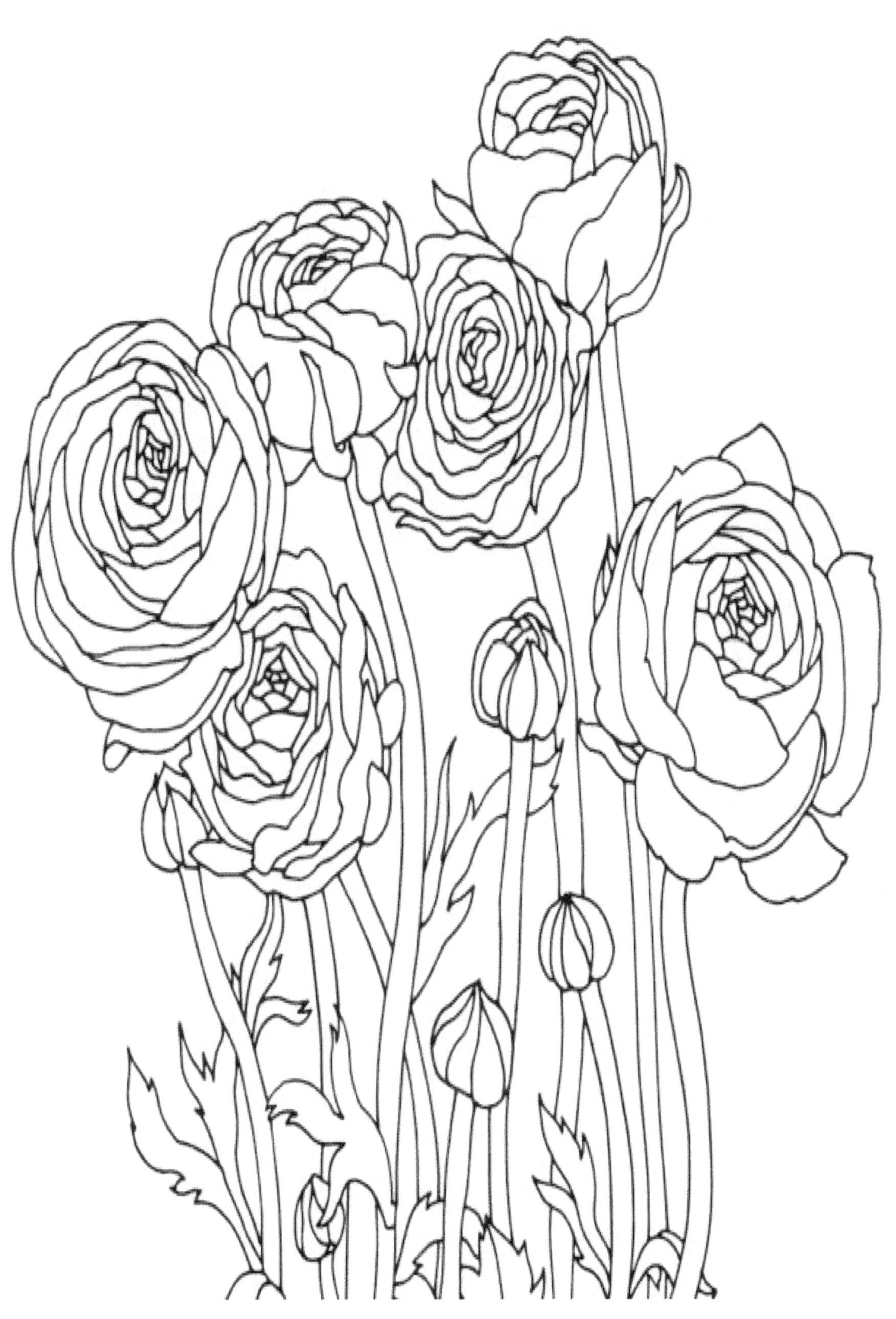

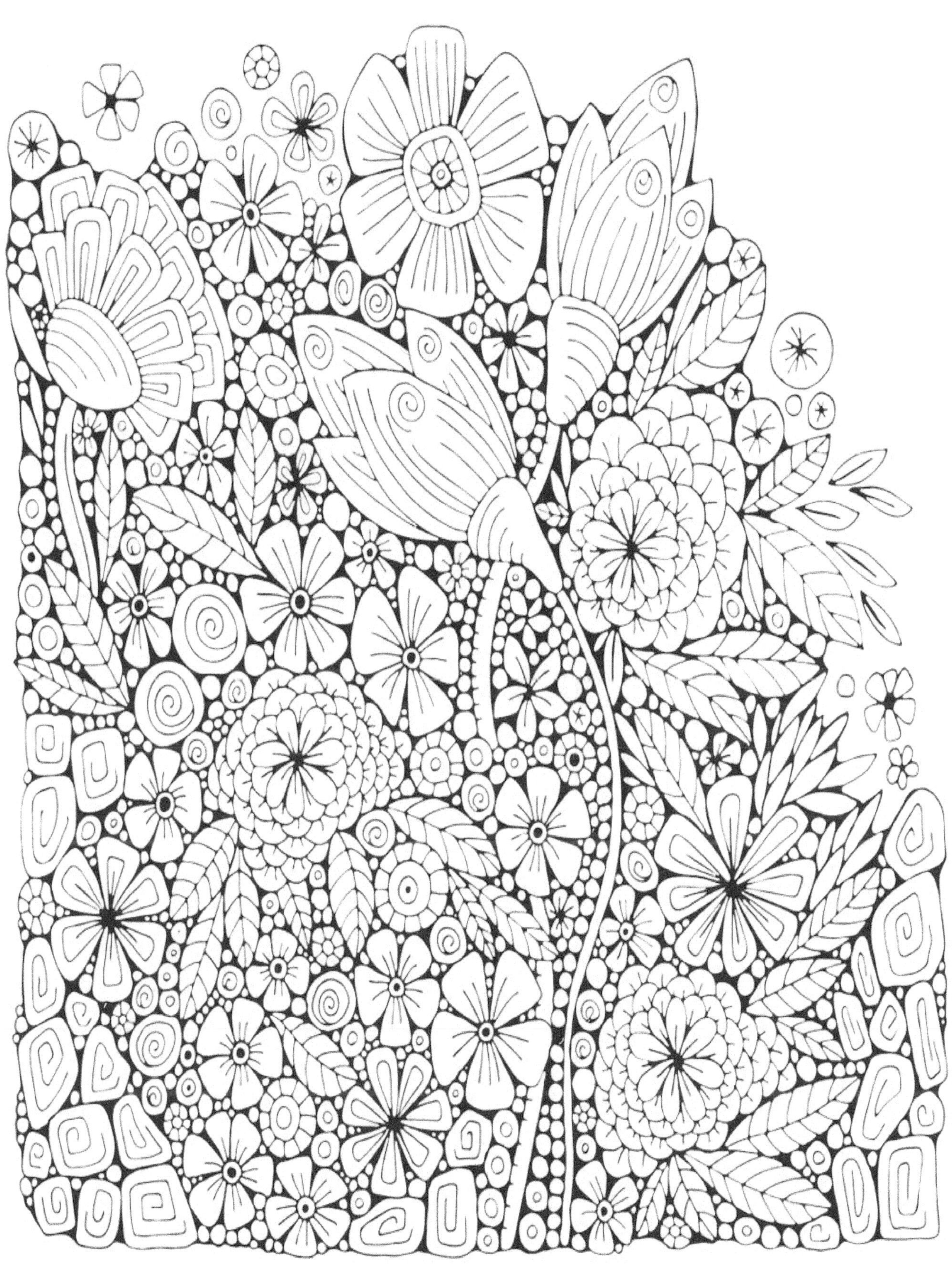

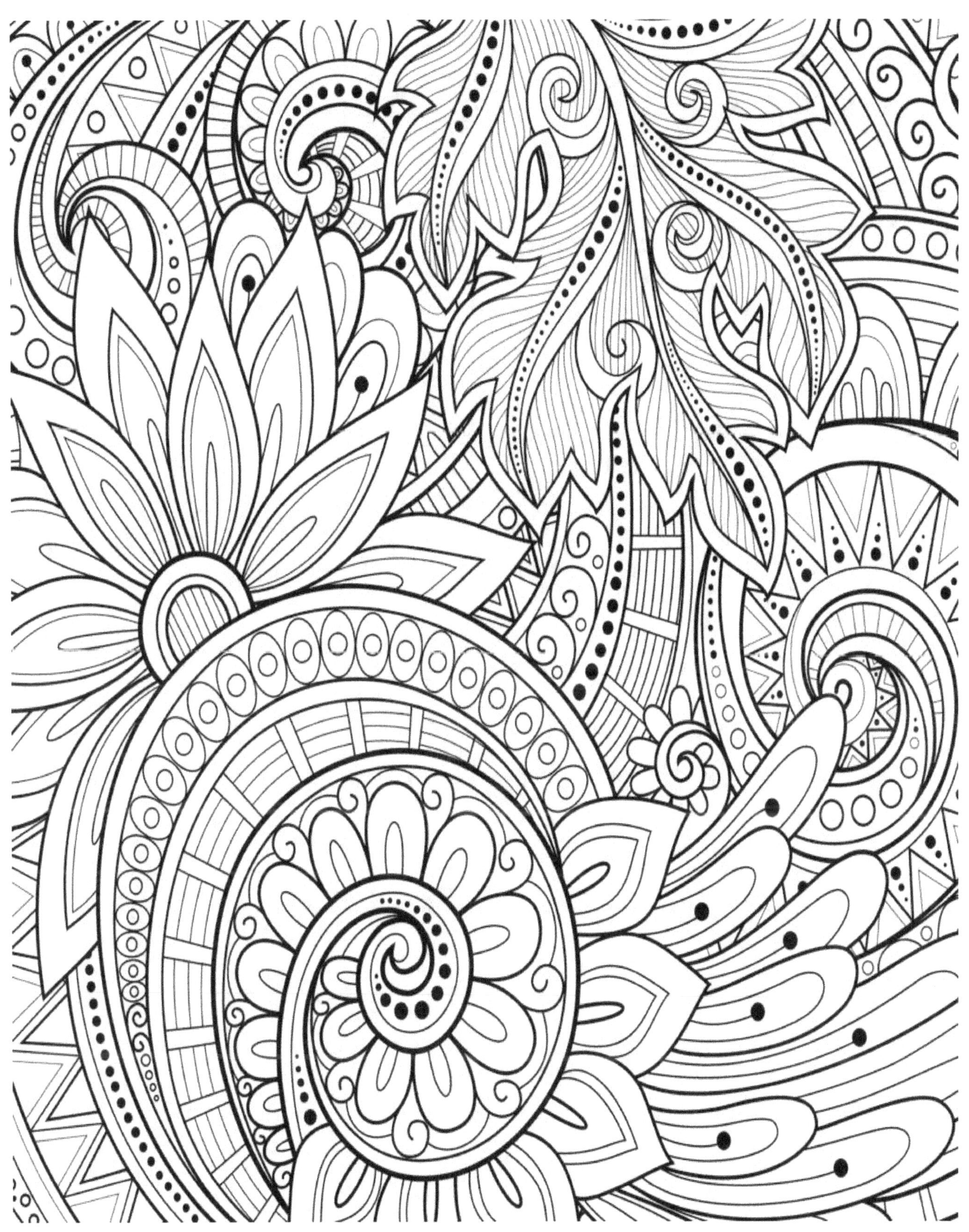

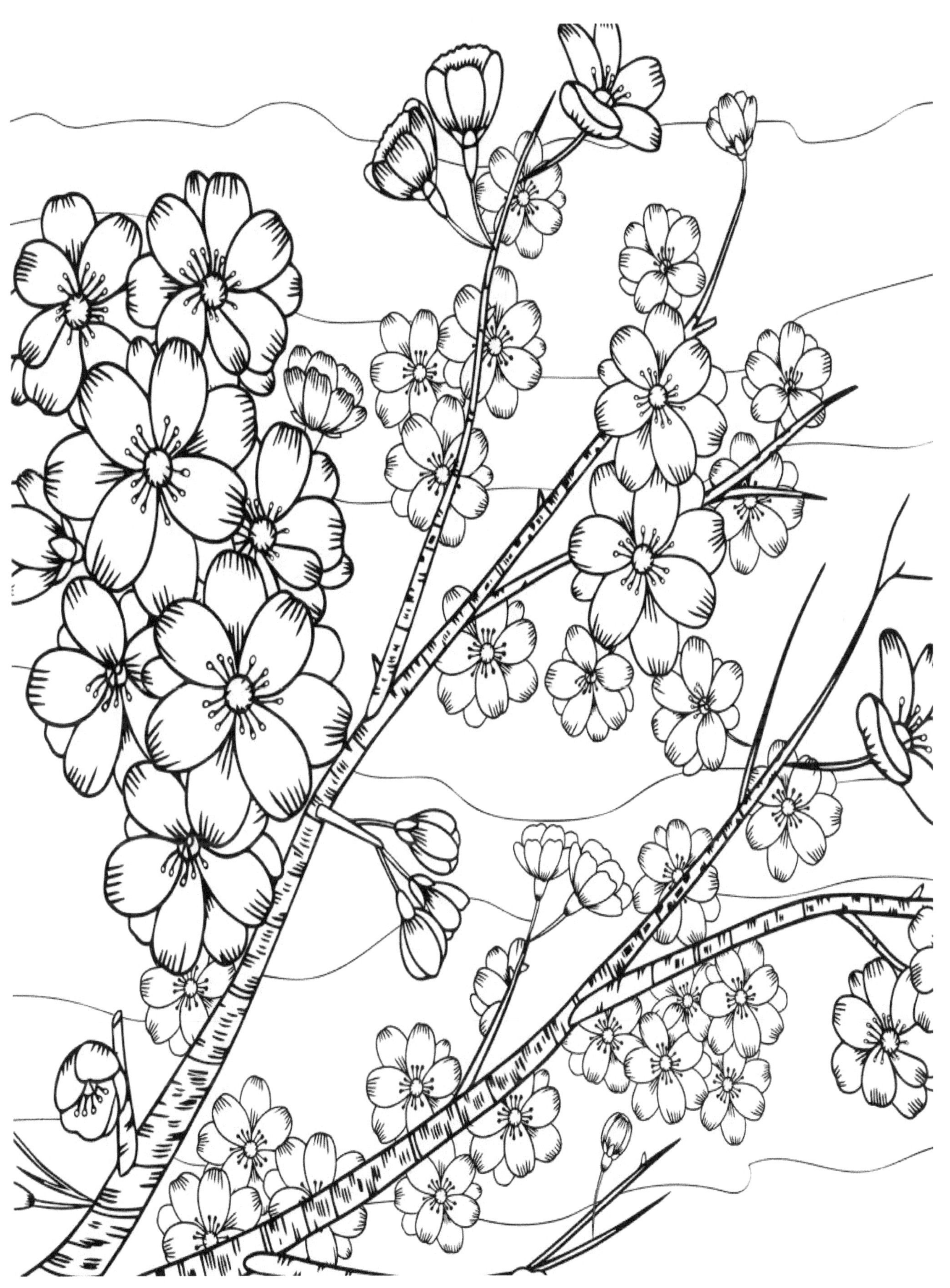

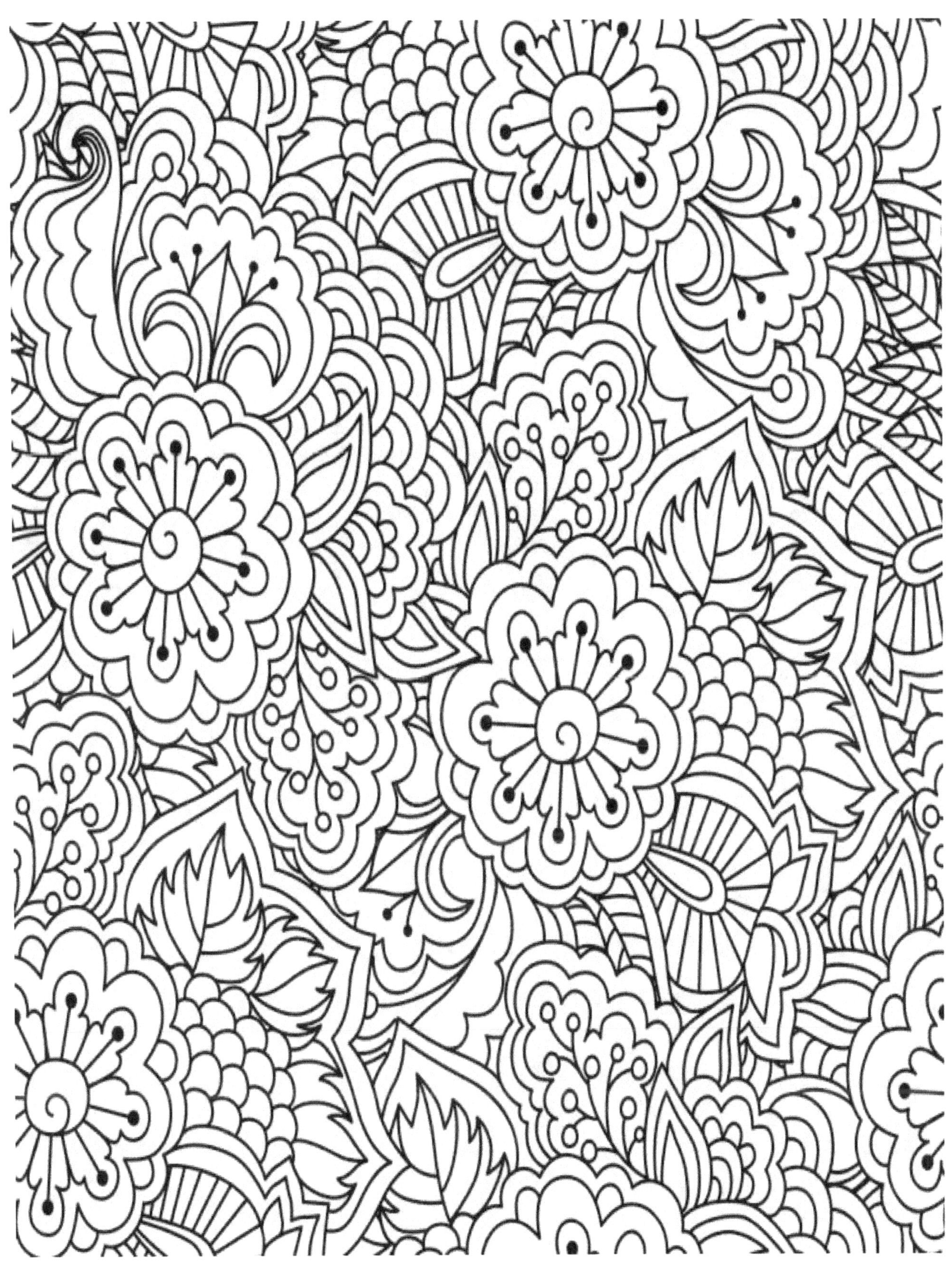

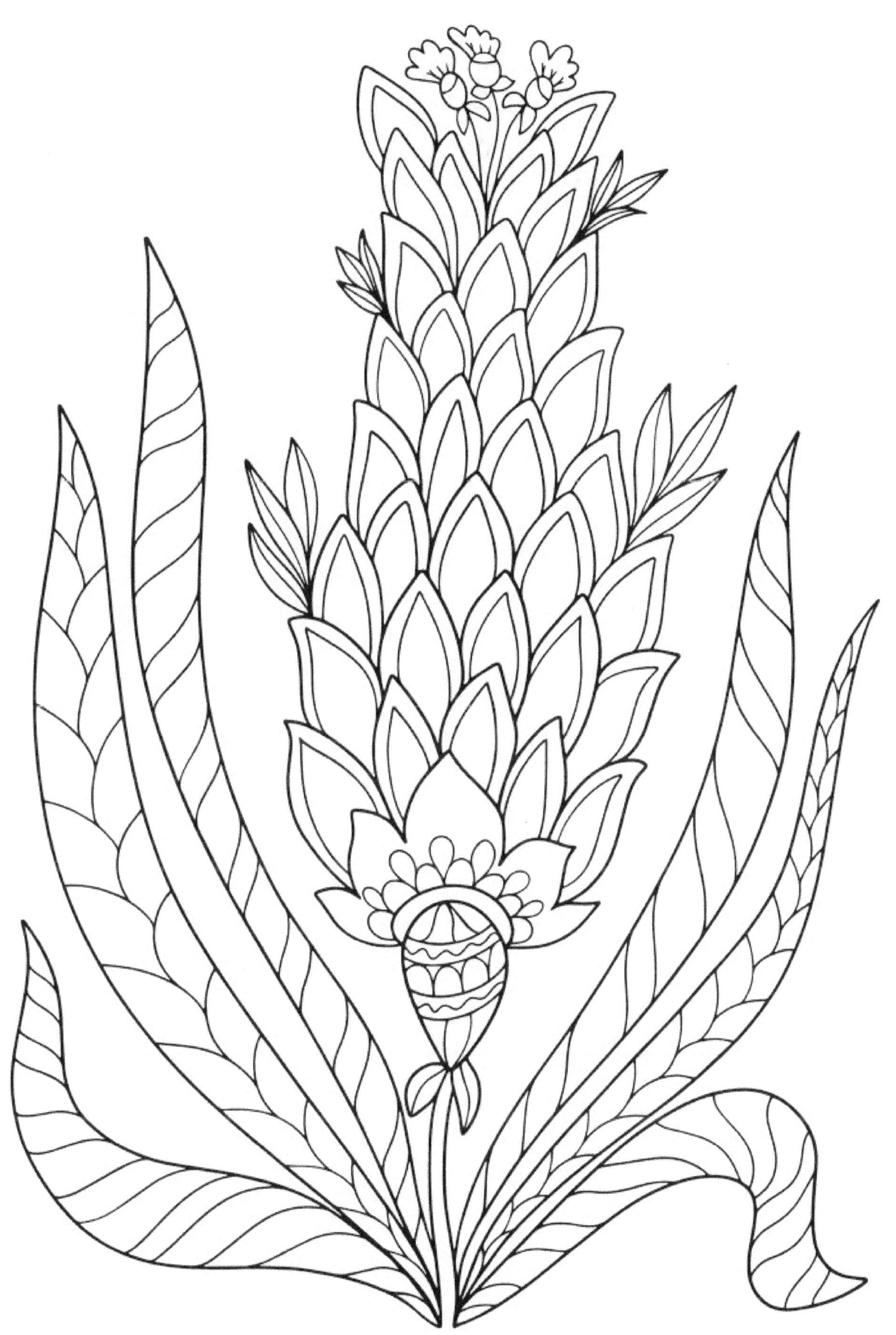

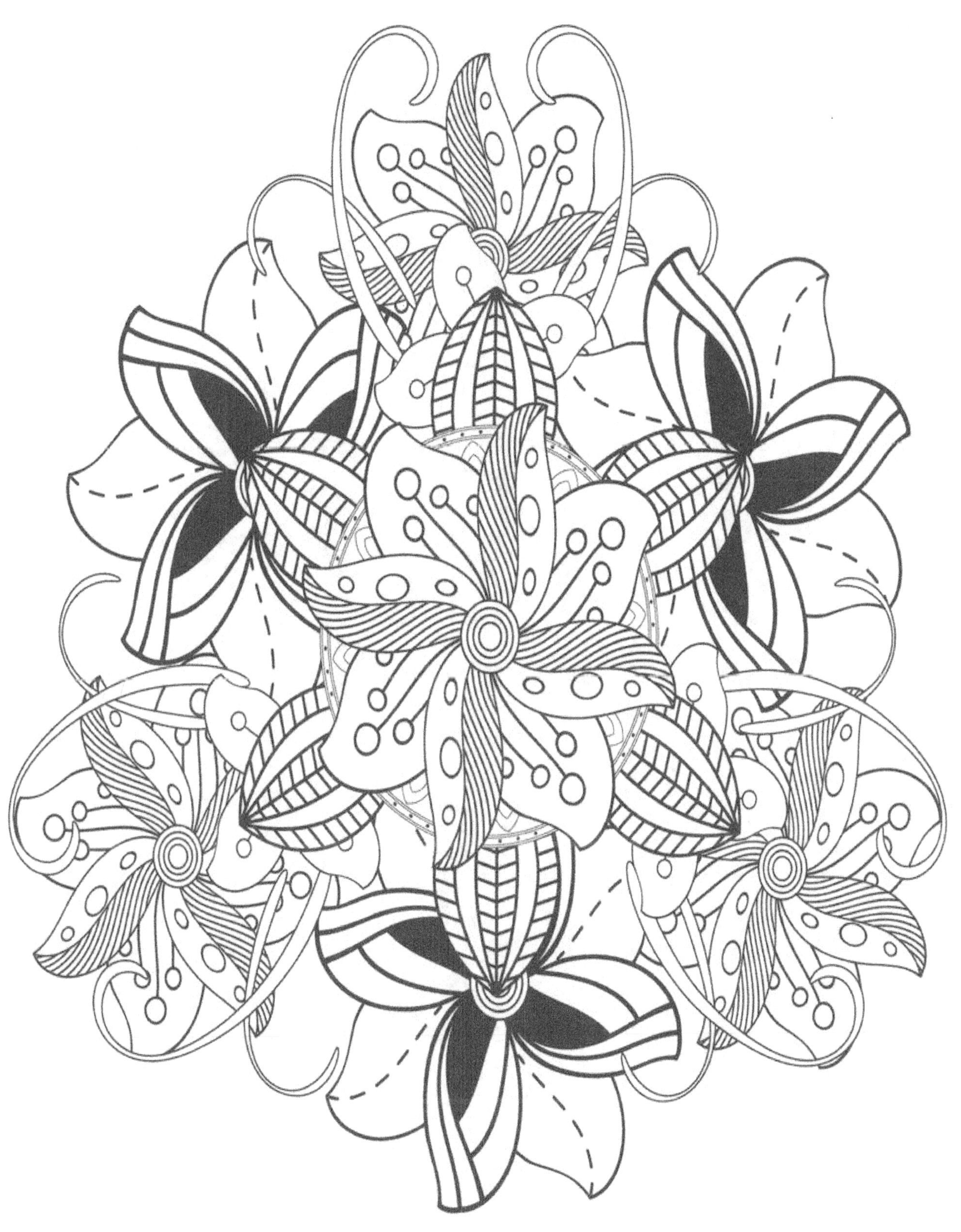

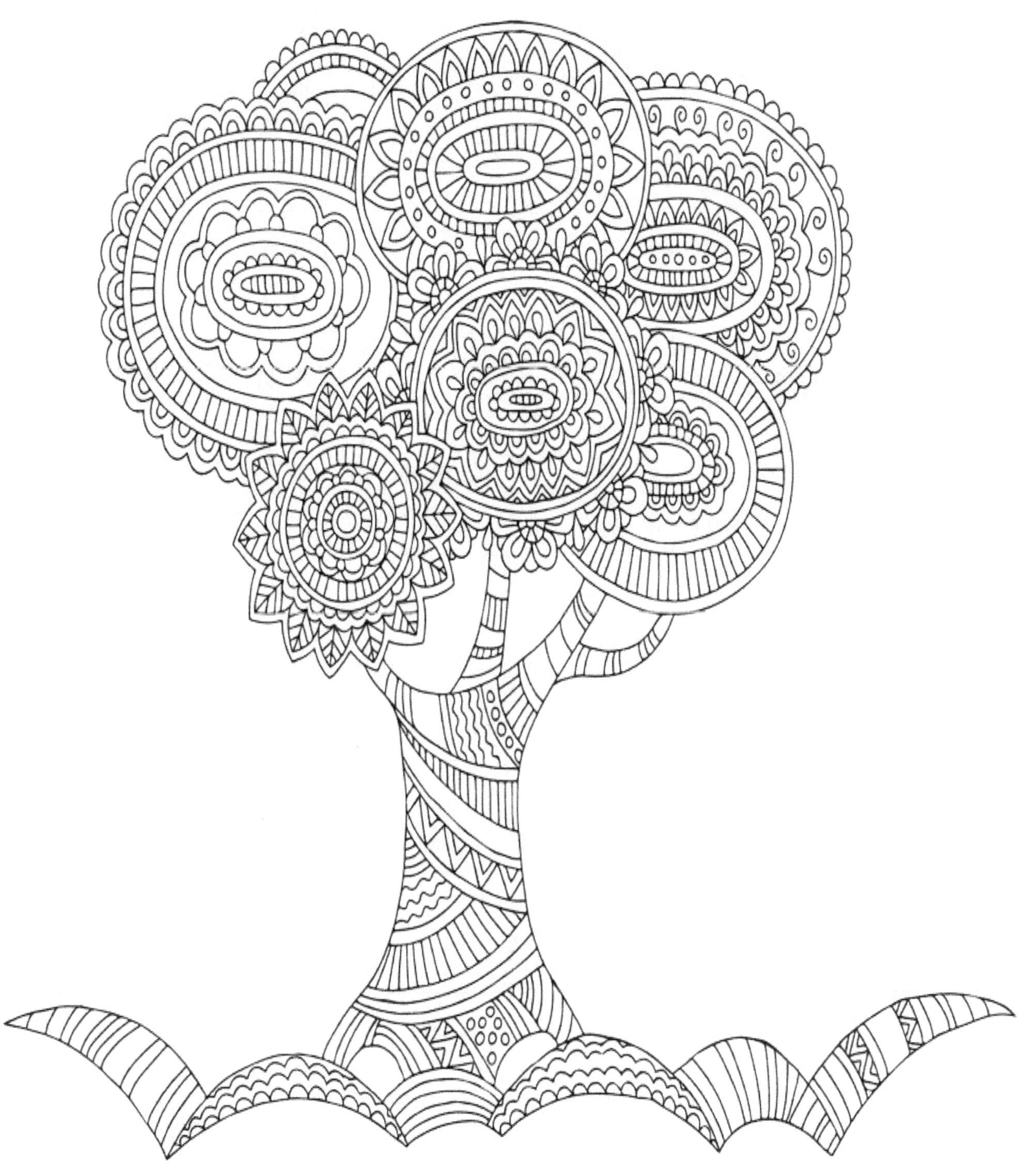

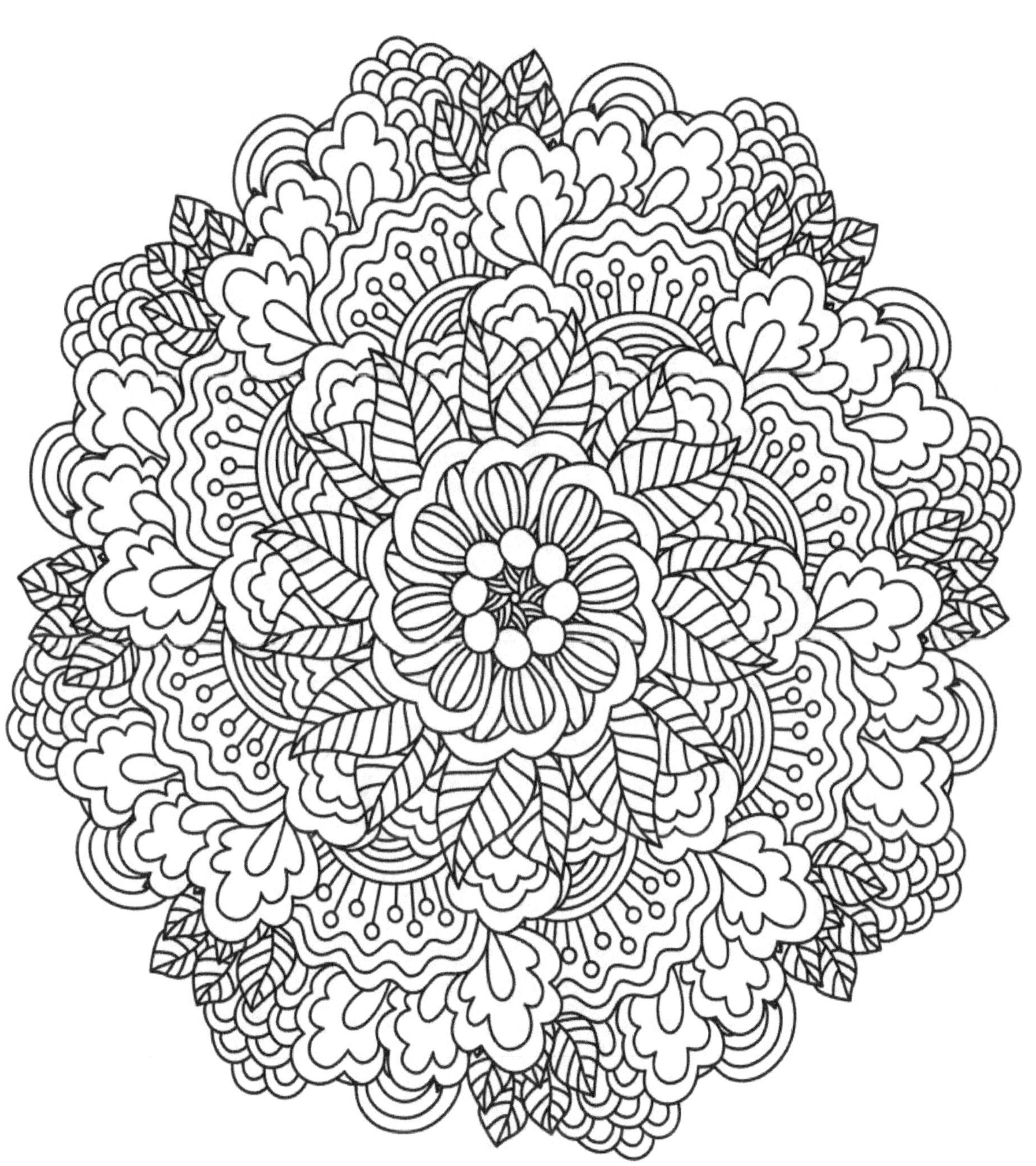

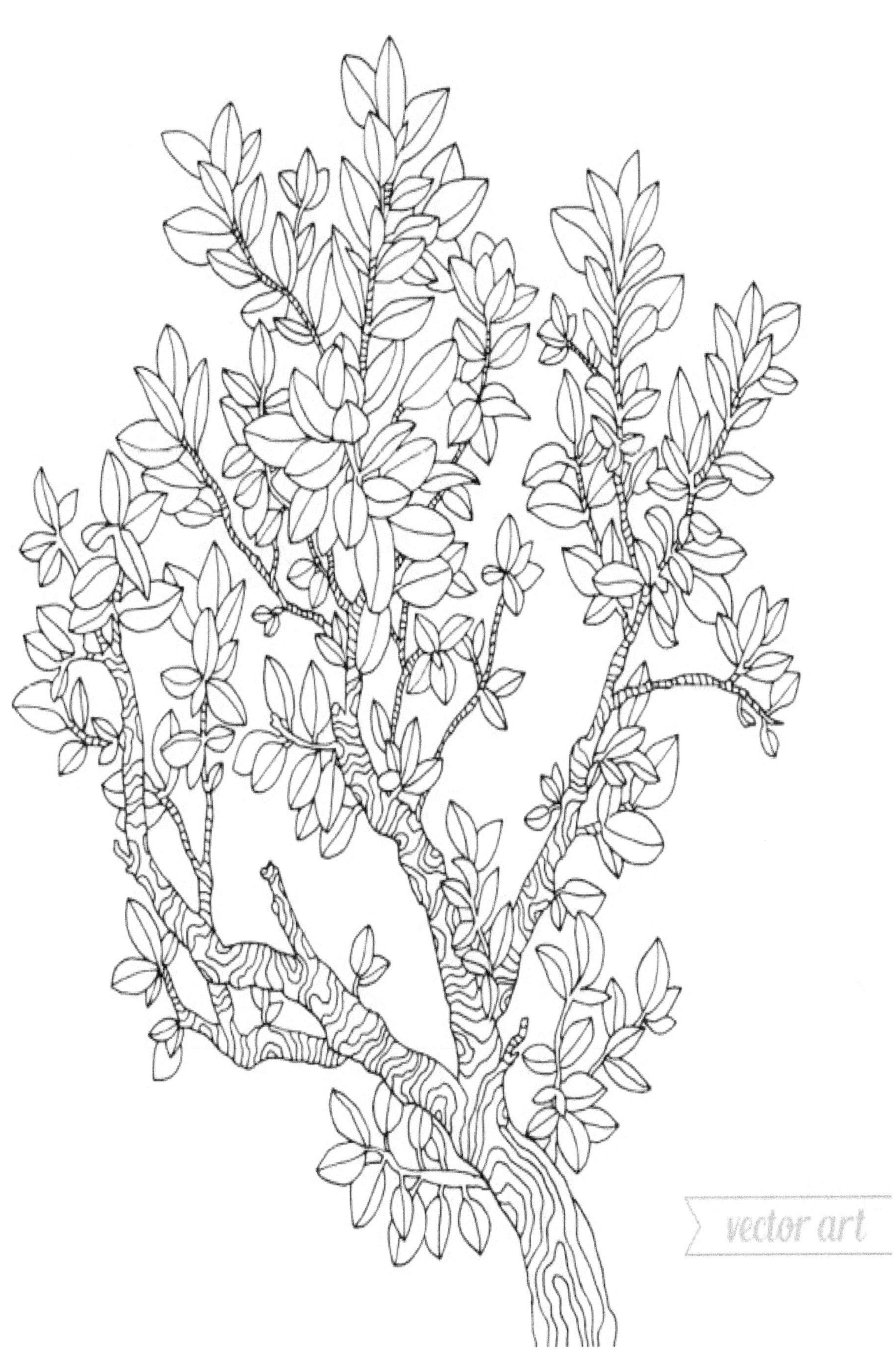
vector art

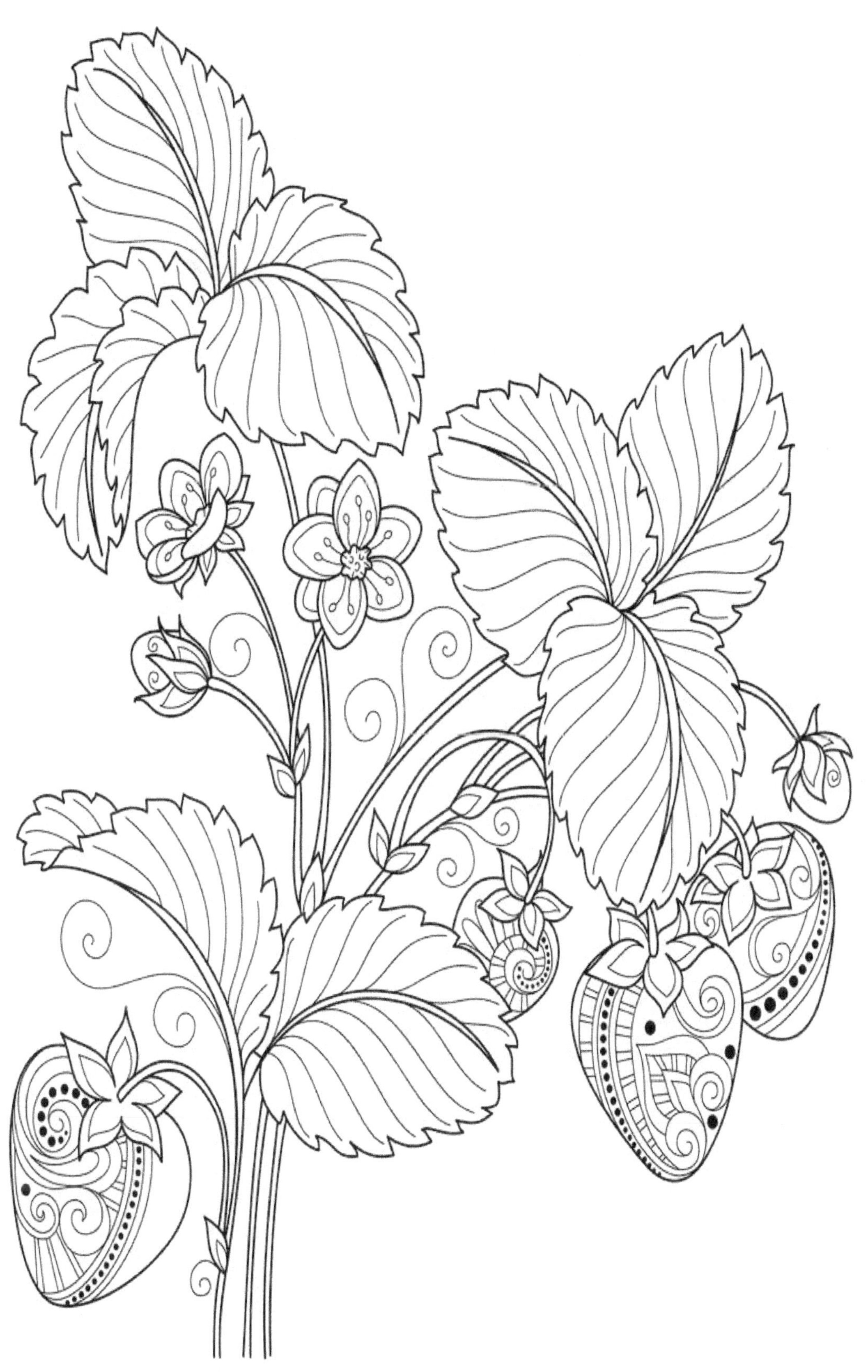

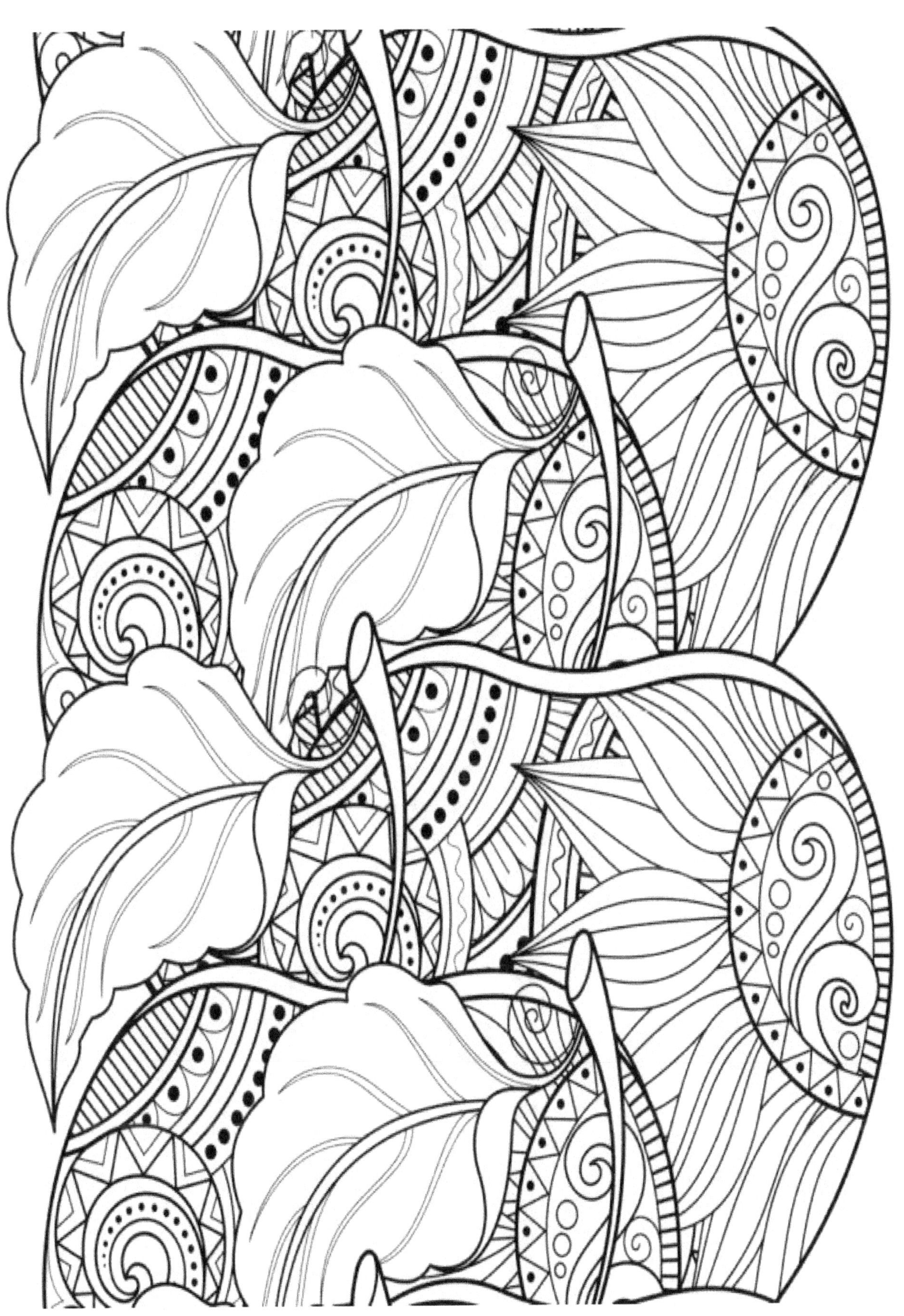

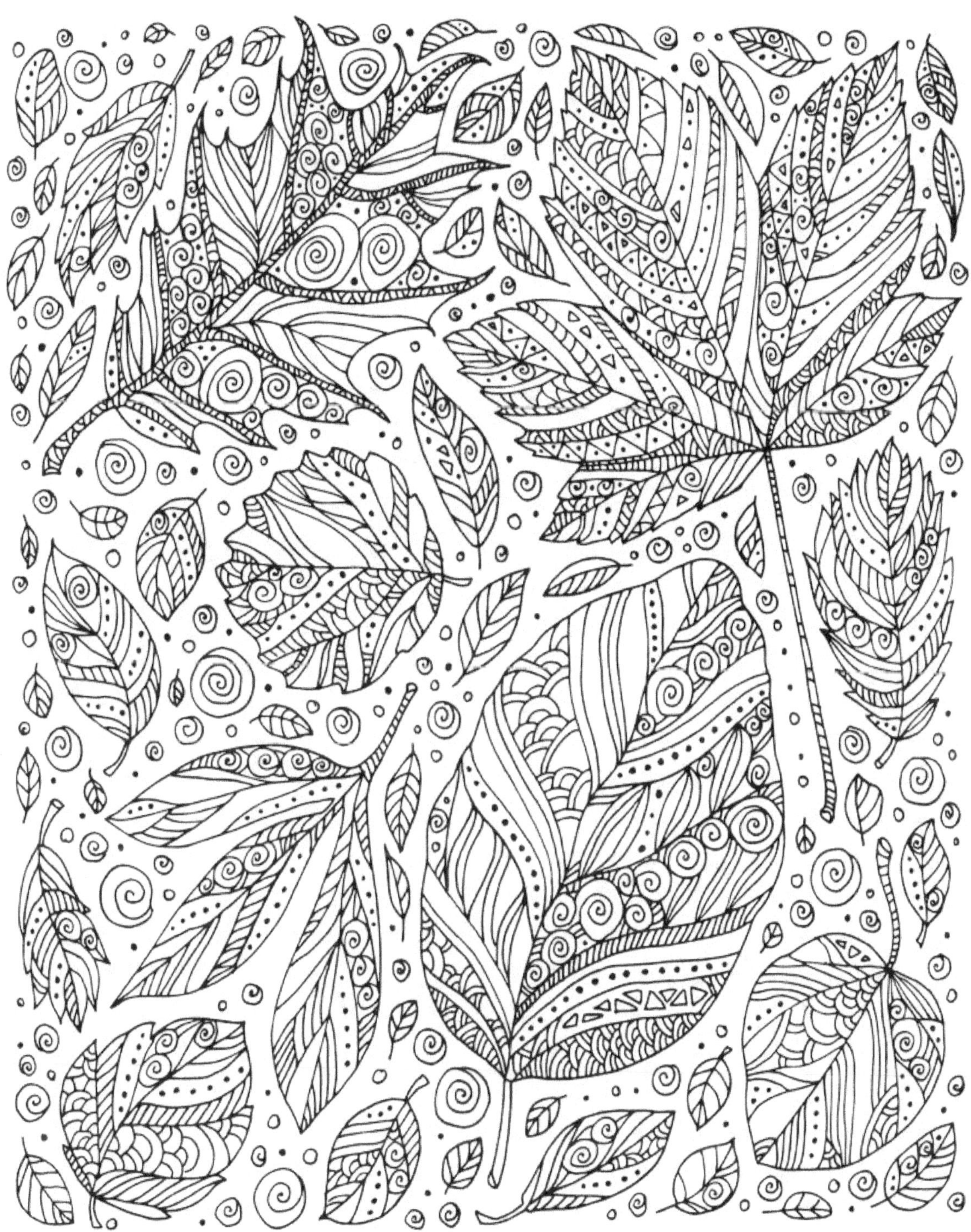

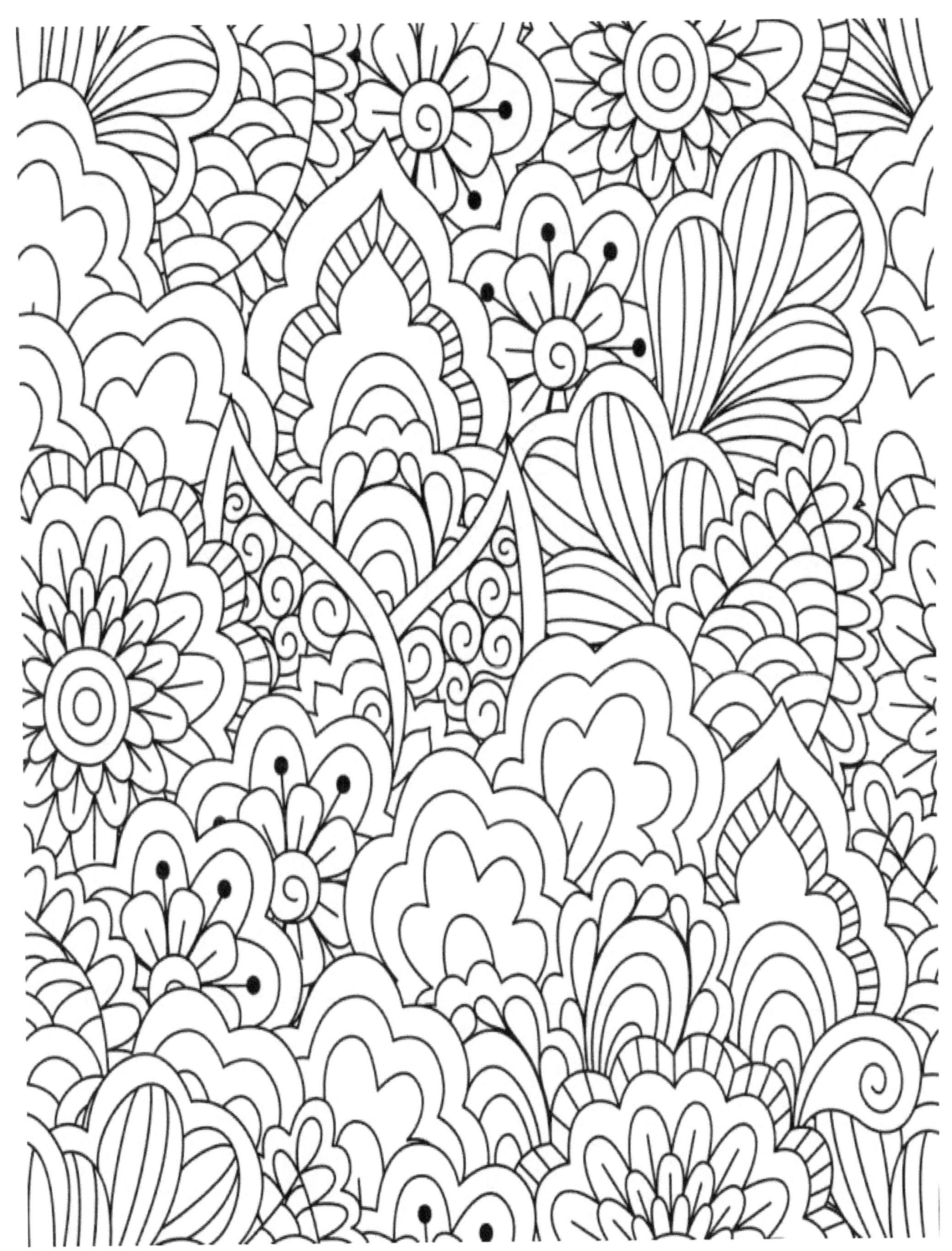

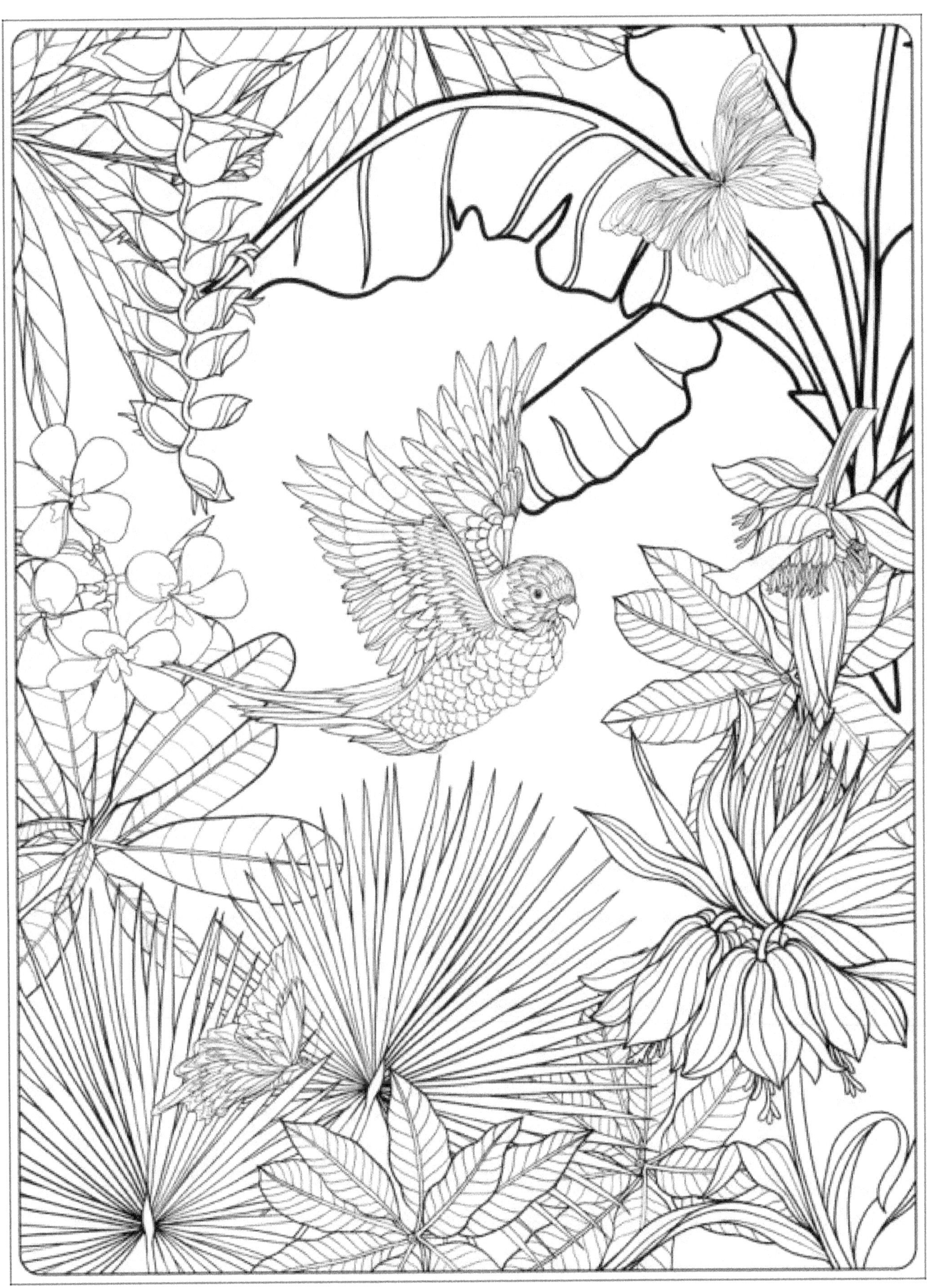

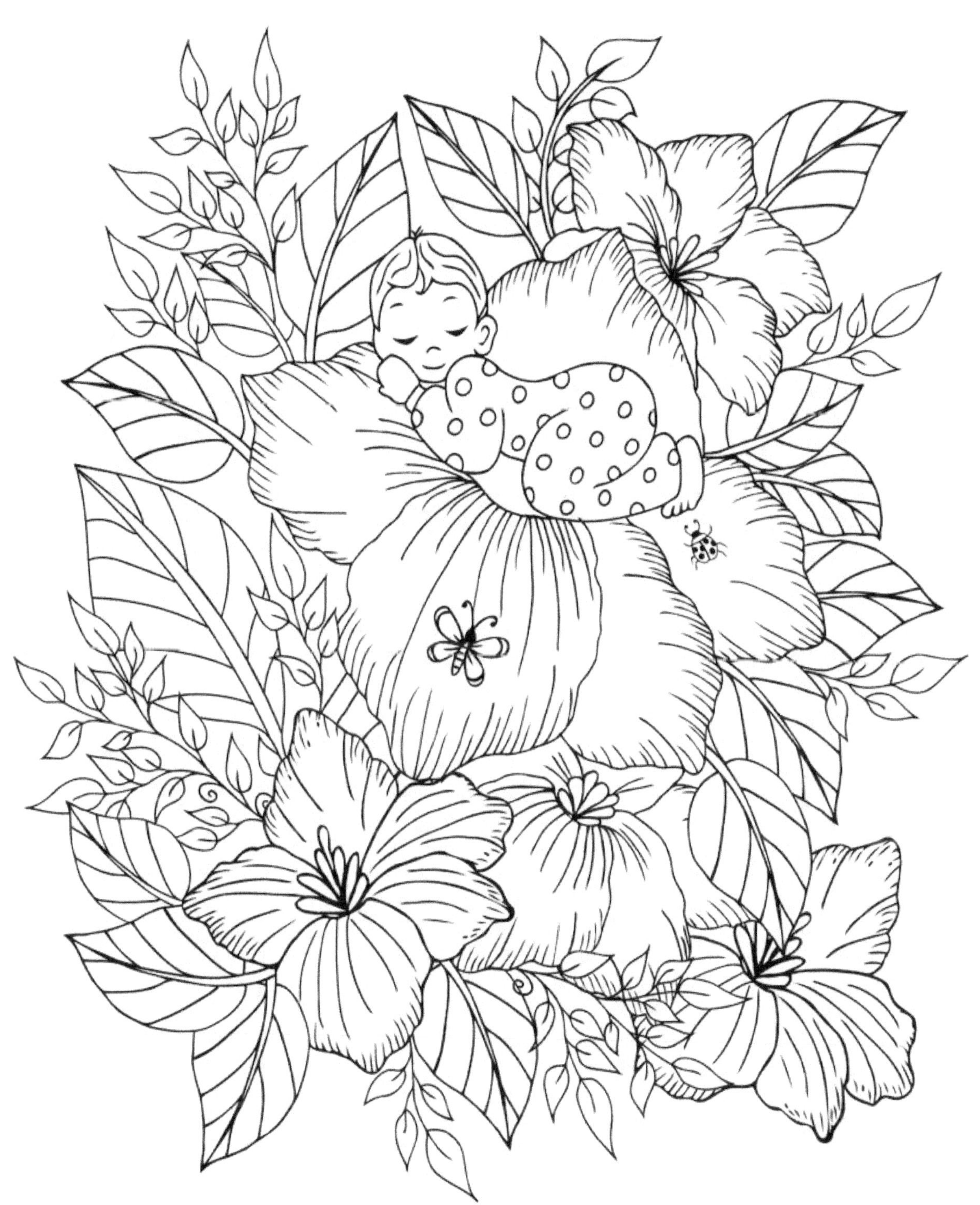

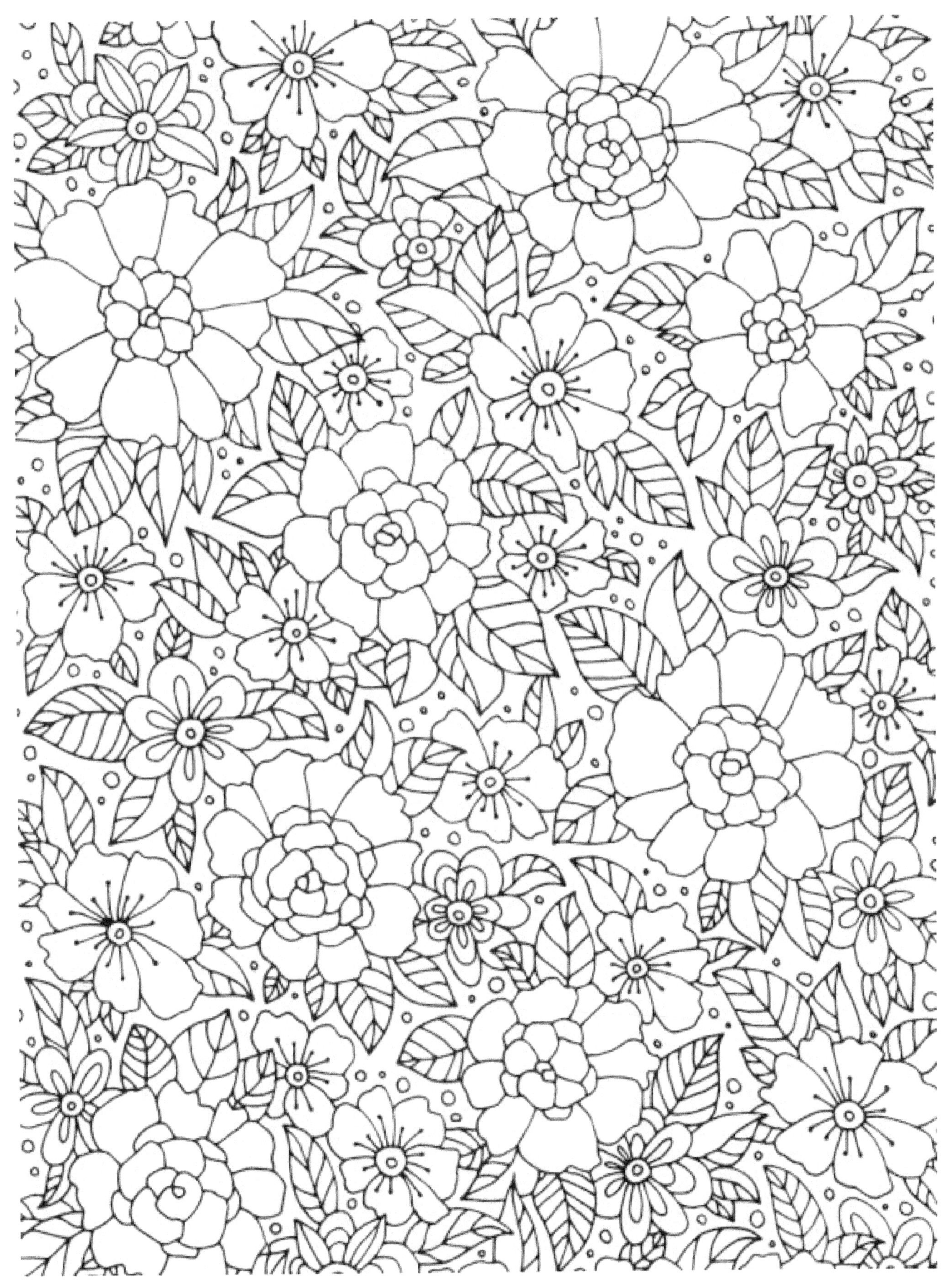

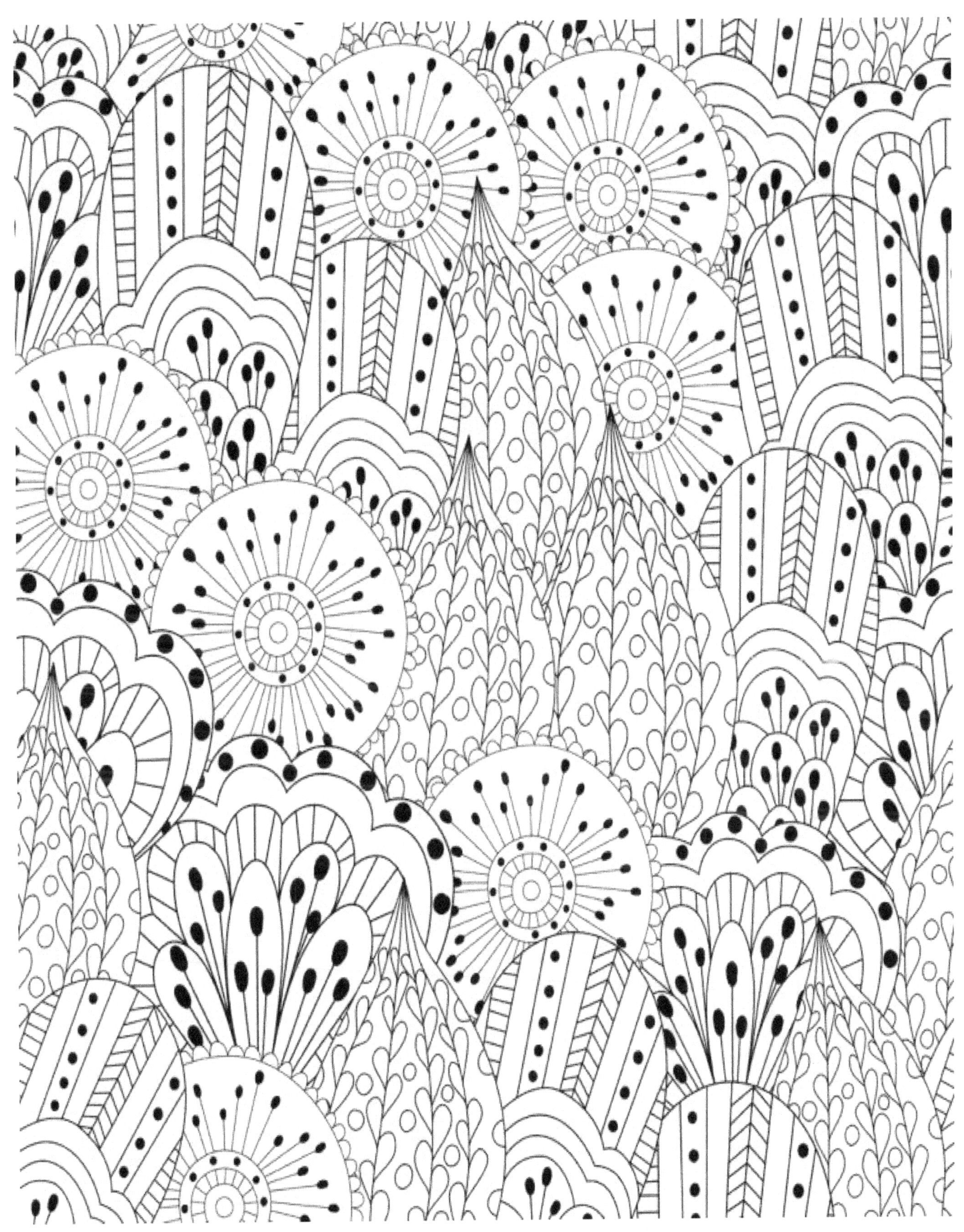

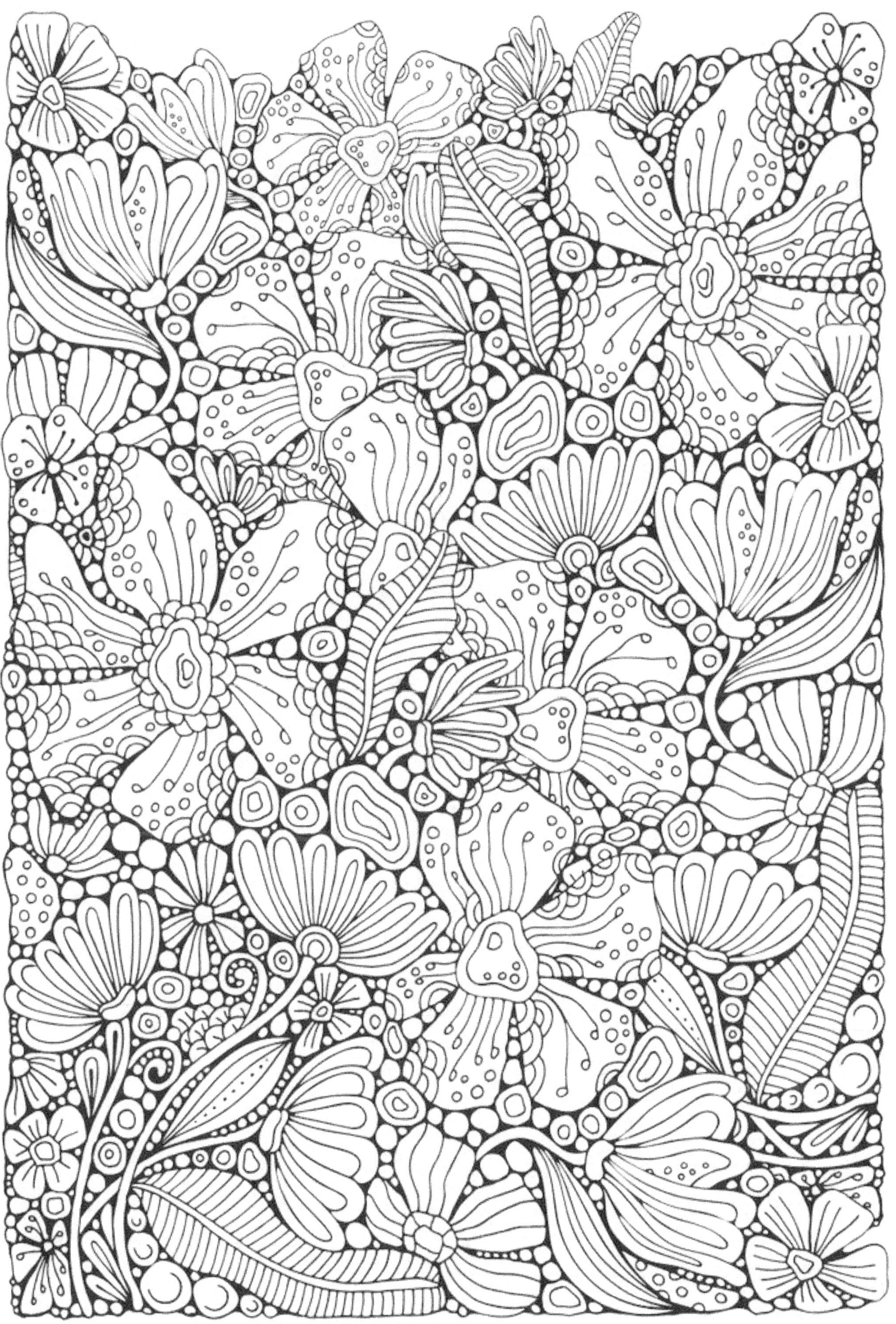

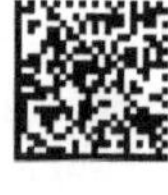